Restoring Order™
to Your Home

Vicki Norris

D1364992

HARVEST HOUSE PUBLISHERS

EUGENE, OREGON

Cover by Terry Dugan Design, Minneapolis, Minnesota

Front and back cover photos © AJ's Studio

RESTORING ORDER™ TO YOUR HOME
Copyright © 2007 by Vicki Norris
Published by Harvest House Publishers
Eugene, Oregon 97402
www.harvesthousepublishers.com

Norris, Vicki, 1973-
Restoring order to your home / Vicki Norris.
        p. cm.—(Restoring order)
    Includes bibliographical references.
    ISBN-13: 978-0-7369-1648-6 (pbk.)
    ISBN-10: 0-7369-1648-2 (pbk.)
    1. Home economics. 2. Orderliness. 3. Christian life. I. Title.
    2. TX147.N83 2007
    640—dc22   2006022913

Printed in the United States of America

07 08 09 10 11 12 13 14 15 / LB-CF / 10 9 8 7 6 5 4 3 2 1

I am blessed to have many amazing people in my life who have believed in me and prayed for me, but the credit for this book ultimately goes to God. He gracefully carried me as I wrote, giving me the humbling, awesome experiences that inspired the words. He helped me to write. He orchestrated the details of a hectic season in my life to ensure that the book was delivered to you. Over and over in my ordinary life, God empowers me to do extraordinary things. He can do the same for you. "All things are possible with God" (Mark 10:27).

Contents

Introduction: Take Back Your Life!   7

Part 1: Organizing That Really Works
  1. The Heart of Organizing   13
  2. A Primer for Tackling Your Projects   23
  3. Customize Your Approach   35

Part 2: Public Spaces
  4. The Kitchen   47
  5. The Family Room   59
  6. The Living Room   69
  7. The Dining Room   79
  8. The Playroom   89

Part 3: Private Spaces
  9. The Bedroom   101
  10. The Bathroom   113
  11. The Laundry or Utility Room   123
  12. The Home Office   135
  13. The Hobby Room   151

Part 4: Storage Spaces
  14. The Closet   165
  15. The Garage   179
  16. The Basement and the Attic   191
  17. The Storage Unit   203

Conclusion: Make Room for Living   213

Introduction:

Take Back Your Life!

Virginia called me today, and she was crying. She has health issues, has put on a lot of weight, and she can't get around very easily. Because of these and other issues, she is getting buried deeper and deeper under her disorganization. The backlog has grown so much that she can barely function in most rooms of her home. Virginia told me she feels demoralized and shameful. As I assured her that lots of other people feel the same way, she asked in a tiny voice: "You mean other people deal with this too?"

Perhaps you aren't as desperate as Virginia, but maybe you too feel overwhelmed and surrounded by your chaos. The walls of your home may seem to be closing in on you. The way you're living and the bad habits your kids pick up can make you feel more guilty every minute. You may not share Virginia's health issues, but maybe your relationships or family is suffering because of household disorganization. Just as I told Virginia today, you are not alone!

Getting organized is not about tidying up or finding a home for things. It's not about having a picture-perfect home that looks as if it should be featured in a magazine. It's also not about storage products; plastic bins and sorters aren't the solution. Ordering your life and your environment is about one thing: reclaiming your life.

I'm a veteran professional organizer, and I've seen just about everything there is to see in disordered homes across America. I want to encourage you that organizing your life will not only liberate you from household chaos; it will give you a fresh start on life. Disorder is siphoning your money, your time, and your mental energies. It may even be tapping you out spiritually, leaving you feeling defeated. Life is too short to live like this, my friend. You are at a crossroads as you hold this book in your hands. Now is the time to take back control of your disordered home and life.

When an army begins to lose ground to the enemy, the soldiers have three choices. They can flee and retreat, they can hold their ground and maintain their position, or they can forge ahead and take back stolen territory. I've been in the trenches long enough to know that the first two options never work for the disorganized person. If you flee your disorganization, it will wait for your return, picking up volume as times goes by. If you simply stay with the status quo, you'll always feel defeated and overwhelmed. The only viable option for people who want to reclaim their homes and their lives is to press into the challenge of tackling their disorganization, retaking ground as they go. I would be honored if you would allow me to boldly go with you into the enemy's camp and take back what your disorder has stolen from you!

For a variety of reasons, you've become trapped by disorganization, and your whole house, or at least a room or two, have taken you hostage. With this book, you can break free and take back one room at a time. I don't want you to end up back in the same jail of disorganization that you feel stuck inside now. Because I want your efforts to last, I have been careful not to offer you silly how-to advice that will only prettify your space but dissolve weeks later. Instead, I will offer you real solutions proven in the real world that fit you and your lifestyle.

Organizing solutions are like battle strategies; there is no "one size fits all" approach. You must consider the nature of the enemy, the territory, and the conditions. You must know the outcome you want and the pace at which you want to achieve it. This book provides a sound discovery process and methodology that will give you a whole new perspective on organizing. If you're not sure it will work for you, consider that this discovery process and methodology is successfully used every day by my team of professional organizers to help our clients attack and conquer their chaos.

This book will help you take back the disorganized public, private, and storage spaces of your home. To gain the most insight and give yourself the best chance to succeed, I recommend you read the book from start to finish. If you don't have time for that, at least read part 1 and then proceed to the chapter of your choice. In some chapters I give you a play-by-play strategy for how I have tackled a certain room and in other chapters I present several considerations, and you can decide which options best fit your life and household. Reading the whole book will give you the most thorough picture of strategies and options for each room of your home.

By reading and applying what you learn, you change your thinking as well as your environment. You'll find that ordering your life starts with you! Instead of delivering formulaic, trite approaches to organizing and conventional wisdom, I will deliver an authentic version of organizing that is built around *you.*

Part 1, "Organizing That Really Works," reveals the heart of true organizing. You'll learn that thoughtful assessment on the front end of your project, coupled with sound strategies, will yield results that are intuitive to you and therefore simple to maintain. I'll teach you how to adapt the organizing process to your unique needs by working within your natural habits, pace, and work style. The following three sections will help you work through every room of your home. You won't want to miss the conclusion, "Make Room for Living," where you'll gain more insight into why organizing matters in your household and your life.

If you've read my first book, *Reclaim Your Life*™…*and Get Organized for Good,* you are in a strong position to swiftly take back territory in your home. If you haven't yet read the first book, I recommend you use it as a forerunner and companion to this book. That way, you can cross-reference the tactics in these pages with the concepts of the first book, supporting the practical advice you're gaining here with the essential organizing framework I present in *Reclaim Your Life.*

Together, we are on an organizing mission. Our mission is to get off the road of good intentions, which has kept you retreating and maintaining your status quo for too long. You've likely been in a holding pattern of disorganization, and together we can move from a reactive position to a proactive one. Prepared with a proper perspective of true organizing, you will conquer space after space as your territory grows and the enemy's shrinks! Is the flame of hope starting to ignite for you? Let's carry it onward to light our way because, my friend, there is always hope! Trade in your guilt, distraction, and fear that disorganization causes and experience true and lasting liberation.

Part One

Organizing That Really Works

Chapter 1: The Heart of Organizing

Chapter 2: A Primer for Tackling Your Projects

Chapter 3: Customize Your Approach

This might be the hundredth book you've bought on the topic of organizing in your continual search for solutions that will finally work. You may be feeling defeated before you even begin. This time will be different. I will tell you the truth about organizing. I'm a seasoned professional organizer, and I know firsthand that the tips, tricks, and conventional wisdom you read about in magazines are counterfeit substitutes for true organizing. My clients have tried them all. All the shortcuts have left them disappointed, disillusioned, and more disorganized than ever. That's because these folks didn't have an authentic perspective of true and lasting order. When their thinking was transformed, they began to restore order, and things began to change.

In "The Heart of Organizing," I'll explain why you should get organized, why your former efforts haven't lasted, and how to embrace a lifestyle of order. In "Primer for Tackling Your Projects," you will become equipped with the same tools my professional organizers use. To ensure that these strategies work for you I show you how to "Customize Your Approach" so that your process fits your life and generates lasting results. Get ready for real change, real results, and real success!

1
The Heart of Organizing

As a professional organizer I have had the unique opportunity to go behind the scenes in people's personal and professional lives. I have seen all the attempts people have made to get organized and have helped figure out why those attempts did not succeed. Like a detective, I use the clues that I find to deduce the factors that contributed to their disorganization. Once I have made these discoveries, I can help my clients resolve their organizational challenges.

A professional organizer wears many hats. I help people figure out what is broken and how to fix it. I am a forensic investigator, process specialist, planning technician, and problem solver. To my clients I become a trusted advisor, advocate, coach, cheerleader, mediator, and confidant. Depending on the client and the unique organizational challenges, I may serve to connect them with other service providers, improve their efficiency, consult on their business issues, and help them manage their lives. Above all, as a professional organizer, I am blessed to be invited into the fabric of other people's lives and entrusted with their problems. I take this trust seriously. For every person or company I serve, either directly or through my organizing consultants, I want to effect positive, sustainable life change.

I've been in the business long enough to know that you simply cannot achieve long-term benefits from your organizing efforts if you have a skewed impression of true organizing, ignore the reasons you are disorganized, or shortcut the restoration process. When you believe organizing is about prettifying your space, for example, you will not experience the benefits of lasting order. If you neglect the introspection that true organizing requires, the success of your efforts will be short-lived. When you view organizing as an activity, you will not experience a transformed life. Because I am so passionate about seeing you come to a freeing knowledge of true order, I want to share with you some worthy reasons to order your life, why you may not have been successful so far, and the only kind of organizing that really works.

Why Get Organized?

We've all heard that we should get organized in order to save time and money. These are likely outcomes of ordering your home, but they are too trite and overused to mean anything anymore. *Why should I get organized?* might be a silly question on the surface. You may be thinking, *I bought a book on organization, I'm obviously interested in getting organized. I don't need to be convinced.* Yet even those who think they want to get organized may not fully understand the true benefits of doing so. Moreover, we sometimes forget our reasons to get organized once we realize it is a long-haul investment. Our reasons like "to make the house look better" quickly dissipate when all our efforts have brought us full circle back to the place we started three weeks ago. If we don't understand the lasting motivators to get organized, we may become disheartened along our organizing journey.

Experience Peace of Mind

One of the immediate results of ordering your environment is peace of mind. When we invest the time, energy, and resources into restoring order to our space, a new clarity arises. When things are sensibly arranged, we can think straight and operate to our highest capacity.

We were designed in order and creativity, and when we are living in sync with our design, we are living as we were intended. A lot of people mistakenly equate being organized with being rigid and lacking creativity. On the contrary, in every instance I've observed, coming out of a state of chaos into a state of order actually renews energy and creativity. Organization actually releases the peace and clarity of mind to concentrate, express creativity, and live abundantly. For more on how living in order can help us to flourish personally and professionally, visit chapter 8 of *Reclaim Your Life.*

Enjoy Harmony in the Home

Some people who call our office for organizing assistance report that their marriages and jobs are on the line because of their disorderly ways. When these folks allow our organizing consultants to help them resolve their messes and mend their ways, the shame and frustration they were feeling recedes. They develop a newfound pride in their environment, make lifestyle changes, and begin to repair their relationships.

As I share in my first book, I see a spiritual connection between our state of order and our quality of life. We were designed in order and meant to live in order so we can experience the best, not the worst of life. As many of us know all too well, disorganization is a distraction and a drain on our lives. When we reclaim order in our households, we actually begin to strengthen personal boundaries, practice better self-management, and release our own potential. As we restore order, family members find more enjoyment in their environment and their relationships, and a new harmony begins to settle over the home.

Live an Example

The home is the incubator of our values and self-image. It is where we learn many of life's lessons and become equipped with skills for successful living. Buried by their clutter and feeling surrounded by their disorganization, many moms call us in a panic. They are fed up with their own inability to cope with their household chaos. They are not only fearing the outcome of their own bad habits, they can see them inexorably being passed on to their children. We don't enjoy facing the results of disorder in our own lives, but seeing other people live with the outcome of our choices is even more painful.

When you make an investment in a lifestyle of order, you are investing not only in your own sanity but also in your children's future. You are choosing to be proactive. You are setting an example of self-control and exercising wisdom. Our children may not do what we say, but they will almost always do what we do. If you cannot get organized for your own sake, perhaps you can for theirs. When you become more organized and model those skills, your children will copy you!

Extend Hospitality

Almost all disorganized households become focused inward. When the home is constantly a disaster, having anyone over is just too much work. Even the thought of entertaining guests can strike fear in the heart of a disorganized homeowner. After all, letting other people see your mess is embarrassing! Once you've established this trend, continuing in it is temptingly easy. Why make the effort to figure out where things should go if you can use the excuse that no one comes over anyway?

Disorganization continues to mount in homes that are focused inward. Family members are faced with an ever-growing volume of clutter and confusion. These distractions cause loss of belongings, arguments, and stress to all who live there. People eventually begin to disrespect their own belongings if they have too many things or if their stuff is lost, broken, and disorganized. Living for a long time inside a terribly disorganized household is, according to many of our clients, like living in a self-imposed jail. Trapped by your own disorder, you may feel helpless to escape this bondage to chaos.

An inwardly focused home is likely to breed inwardly focused inhabitants. Focusing on yourself and your own problems, needs, and desires is natural when you're busy trying to survive. This self-focus keeps you from noticing and serving the needs of others. How can we give of ourselves when our environment and lifestyle have drained from us every last ounce, and we have nothing left to give?

Being available to minister to others who are in need is the spirit of hospitality. Cultivating a spirit of hospitality is almost impossible in a chaotic, frantic home. Yet we are asked to use the gifts we have received (including our homes and our talents) to reach out to others who are in need (Romans 12:13; 1 Peter 4:9).

When your home is transformed from chaos to peace, you want to invite people inside! You want others to experience the long-awaited peace you now enjoy. After order is restored, your home feels like a sanctuary that you can open up to others. Organizing your home can release your desire and ability to practice the spirit of hospitality by switching your inward focus to the needs of others.

Live Your Priorities

The most important result of ordering your home is the relief you will feel when you are no longer letting yourself down on a daily basis. Living a haphazard, disorganized life creates stress and has many consequences. From losing things to missing deadlines, disorderly living is one disappointment after another. When you are constantly living out of step with your values because you are in survival mode, your lifestyle is not in congruence with your true priorities. When you restore order to your home, you slow down your frantic pace and come into sync with your own values.

Living according to our priorities will look a little different for every one of us. Priorities, unlike goals, don't change from season to season; they are constant values we hold dear. Investing in your marriage is a priority. Being an engaged parent is a priority. Investing in your dreams (either personal or professional) is a priority. Sadly, our priorities are usually shoved to the back burner when we live chaotic lives. We barely have enough time and energy to keep our heads above water, let alone invest in the things that matter to us.

I am passionate about organizing, but not because it makes people's homes and offices look nice, and not because of the neat containers and products. I am passionate about helping people bring their lives into orderly focus precisely because I want them to discover and embrace the things that really matter in this world. I want you to be free to live out your true priorities.

Why Haven't You Been Able to Get Organized?

Conventional wisdom tells us that organizing is simply "a place for everything and everything in its place." Our built-in drive to find a quick fix tells us that organizing must be about storing our stuff in plastic bins. Yet I think we all know that the reason we resist organizing is that deep down we know it is not simplistic, it's not a quick fix, and it isn't about the products.

When Kari first started her organizing project, she told me she just had a paper problem. Paper was piling up in her kitchen, on the ledge inside the front door, and in the home office. She was constantly running late paying her bills. When I interviewed her, I discovered that Kari didn't just have a problem with paper; she had a problem managing her time. Kari was never at home. She worked long hours, and when she did get home late at night she had to fix dinner and do enough laundry to get her through the week. All she had time to do was scoop up the mail and deposit it on the nearest surface.

Sure, Kari needed help establishing a system for processing paper and a good filing system, but more importantly, she needed to take back control of her time. As you can see, if we had simply just "tidied up" Kari's problem and given her a few paper systems, her newfound "order" wouldn't have lasted very long because it wouldn't have been supported by proper time management.

We sat down together and talked about Kari's schedule. Together, we realized she was working 70 hours a week. No wonder she couldn't get to the bills! Even she was shocked when she examined how she was truly spending her time. We set a more rational schedule for Kari, which included a daily processing time for her to read and deal with mail and pay bills. Then, we scheduled three back-to-back days to tackle her home office and establish the necessary systems. When we were all done with her project, Kari not only had paper management systems in place, she had begun to adjust to a more balanced life.

Like Kari, you are going to need to figure out what is really behind your disorganization. Sometimes what appears to be causing your problems is only the tip of the iceberg. I look at the whole person and his or her lifestyle to understand the issues we need to work on together. Rather than just dealing with the symptoms of the problem, we need to discern the malfunction that is causing the problem!

Needing to improve your time management or stop a compulsive shopping habit that is causing household disorder may seem fairly obvious, but self-defeating behaviors can be hard to recognize in ourselves. We also must look at the background of our disorganization as well, just as if we were looking into our medical history. In chapter 3 of *Reclaim Your Life,* you can learn about situational, habitual, historical, social, and chronic disorganization. Every day, I see these five causes of disorganization contributing to my clients' frustration. Until you diagnose the reasons behind your struggle with disorganization and address them, your organizational efforts will likely be short-lived at best. If you are ready and willing to address your faulty thinking and self-defeating behaviors you are a candidate for lasting success in your organizing journey!

Organizing Is a Lifestyle

Picture yourself pulling out a nasty weed of disorganization by its roots and triumphantly tossing it in the recycle bin. Instead of just lopping off the top, you need to dig down and uproot that pernicious weed. If you invest the time to dislodge its spindly threads and work it out of the soil, you will have conquered that weed and halted its attempt to take over your yard.

Yet what happens when you look up from that one weed and survey the rest of your property? You will likely see more weeds ahead. Most of us don't have only one messy room. If you just have one issue with disorganization, you are in the blessed minority. Most of us struggle with various issues in our space, time, and paper. Figuratively speaking, most people I know have an entire yard filled with weeds of disorder that need to be pulled. When your property has been infested with weeds, you must pull them out one at a time and then apply some weed prevention. This obviously takes a healthy dose of both time and commitment.

True organizing, like weeding, is not a one-time activity that yields instant and permanent results. When you go to the supermarket and see the magazines promising "order in a hurry" or "three simple steps" to get organized, just remember that those are nothing more than short-term shortcuts. We've all been disillusioned by those shortcuts in the past. Later we realized that the shortcuts can only deliver the *appearance* of order; they don't really solve our problems. Because you're reading this book, I'm guessing you really want to experience something you haven't yet been able to achieve: long-lasting change. If you can see the common sense in rejecting organizing as a quick-and-dirty fix, you will be on your way to discovering the heart of true organizing.

Organizing is not an activity; it is a process that takes time, introspection, and change. If you embrace organizing as a process that you are beginning now and will stay committed to over time, you can achieve victory over your weeds of disorder. Even after you pull out a weed by its roots, you will find another one to dislodge, and after you've eliminated that one, you will need to maintain the weed-free soil. Try not to look at this as a futile process. If you've ever weeded an infested yard and started gaining on the problem, you know the satisfaction that comes from seeing the fruits of your labor. You know that an investment like this takes time, but eventually you gain on those weeds, and they don't come back as frequently or in the same quantity as before. Consistent organizing will yield the same satisfaction of gaining on the enemy and taking back stolen territory.

Diligent weeding will also protect your grass and plants from being infiltrated by weed intruders. Weeds have a way of choking out healthy plants, robbing them of life and circulation, and that is exactly what disorganization will do in your home. Disorder will clog the flow of your household, and if left unchecked, will choke out the healthy functioning of your home. My friends, this is why you must get organized: to regain control from the weeds of disorganization in your life.

Organizing and maintaining your home is a new lifestyle you are assuming, not a quick fix. Like weeding, it is a two-part process. First, you must tackle backlog…all that stuff or paper that has been building up and choking out your peace of mind. A backlogged home is like a weed-infested field. As you are attacking your backlog you may need some help with options and ideas, and that is where this book will come in handy.

Second, after you have the backlog under control you will want to set up systems to help you manage incoming items and paper. You will want to clarify the purpose of each space in your home and have a plan for routing and dealing with new stuff. In these pages you will learn how to roll out your project in phases, avoid common pitfalls, and consider the best systems for your life.

To gain victory over the disorganization weeds you will need to dig out from the backlog, set up systems that fit your life, and maintain what you've established. Like a vigilant gardener who keeps up her efforts to protect her hard work, you will gain momentum as you go and become more committed as you progress. When you pull the weed of disorganization out by its roots, you will begin to reap the benefits and joy of an orderly home.

Organizing your life is not a Band-Aid; it's an antidote that, applied daily, will remedy your problem and prevent it from recurring. Disorganization can be remedied; I've seen it happen over and over again, and it can happen for you too! It's not a quick fix; it's a set of customized solutions that work. I have seen small organizing projects and epic-sized disasters, and every single one is surmountable with the correct perspective and methodology.

Once you understand that the true heart of organizing is about gaining your own freedom, not applying another tired trick, you will begin to claim this process for yourself. Join me in moving through your household room by room and beginning the rewarding process of establishing true and lasting order.

2

A Primer for Tackling Your Projects

Wʜᴀᴛ sᴇᴘᴀʀᴀᴛᴇs sᴜᴄᴄᴇssꜰᴜʟ ᴏʀɢᴀɴɪᴢɪɴɢ from not-so-successful organizing? Why do your organizing efforts often bring you full circle back to the place where you began? Often, our efforts to get organized are just mad attempts to eliminate our chaos once and for all. We think that if we could just get it right this time we'd never have to organize again.

Unfortunately, that's not the way true organizing works. As we discussed in the previous chapter, successful organizing is a lifestyle, not a one-time activity. True organizing is an ongoing process that includes dealing with the backlog that has been accumulating and setting up systems to help you manage in the future. Not-so-successful organizing is characterized by taking shortcuts and haphazardly applying tips and tricks. You can experience lasting change and success if you embrace an authentic view of organizing.

I want to share with you the methods our professional organizers use to tackle any organizing project. These tactics work just as well in a professional setting as they do in the home environment. Our strategies are designed to scale to each client's needs and scope of project.

We engage our clients in a discovery process. Then we dig in, roll up our sleeves, and begin the physical process alongside them.

Organizing is as much about the change in thinking as it is about the change in environment. We often devalue the mental, emotional, and spiritual elements of the discovery process because we are so conditioned to link organizing to physical transformation. Yet without the discovery process and self-awareness that results, our organizing efforts will prove disappointing and short-lived.

Throughout our work with a client we are creating systems designed with his or her unique needs in mind. People often ask me how they can maintain their systems once they are established. You will be far more likely to maintain a system if it is simple and is created around the way you think than if it is complex and only makes sense to someone else. Of course, to maintain your systems you will also likely have to practice new habits to support the infrastructure you've worked to establish.

Engage in a Discovery Process
Intake Assessment

We begin our work with every client by sitting down and talking. This conversation with the client will be the foundation for all our work. We take notes on our discoveries that we will later share with the client. I wish I had a more glamorous name for this all-important first step, but we simply call it the intake assessment.

Management consultants everywhere use some type of initial assessment to get a baseline for their clients. It is an opportunity for the clients to download their situations in as much or as little detail as they care to share. Our clients usually open up freely with us and share the state of their lives and what makes them tick. This baseline helps us take a client's pulse in the areas of interest. Our organizers are interested in learning about a client's personal and professional life and the scope of his or her organizing challenges.

Set a Timeline and Expectations

We first establish the client's timeline and expectations for her work with us. If the client's mother-in-law is coming for a visit at the end of the month, the timeline to organize the guest room may be short, and she may need a rapid series of appointments. If the client has a whole house project, however, we can help her establish the realistic expectation that she will need to devote time and consistent effort to move through the project.

Expectations are the glue of our relationships with clients. If they think we are going to jump out of our cars, sprinkle fairy dust on their houses, and in four hours create a scene that sparkles with order, we must give them a realistic view of what is possible in four hours of work. If they worry we are going to force them to throw away things they want to keep, we have to correct that faulty thinking and any other fears they may have.

You can start your organizing project by setting a realistic (note that this word keeps being repeated!) timeline for dealing with backlog and establishing systems. Take the time to review your own expectations and ensure they are in line with the nature of true organizing. If you truly expect yourself to organize an entire room in one evening, or tackle the whole house in your week long vacation from work, you may be disillusioned. I've found that most rooms take between 12 and 24 hours to organize thoroughly. Of course, you can tidy a room in far less time than this, but in chapter 1 we noted the difference between tidying up and organizing.

Consider Stakeholders

Our organizers also want to know who the stakeholders are in the organizing project. You can do this for yourself as you consider your organizing project. Is your spouse giving you the reins and asking you to set up the systems that he will then acquire? (Not likely.) Or does your spouse have his own particular needs and preferences that you must consider? (Almost certainly.)

Determine who the decision makers are as you consider each project. If your husband manages the finances, for example, his visual needs and preferences for filing and paper management should be at the heart of those financial systems so they are intuitive for him. If you manage the children and the household, those systems can be built around the way you think. As your children age, you can empower them with more self-management and responsibility by adapting your household systems to the way they think. *Each user* of each system should be considered during the setup phase. Determining stakeholders and involving them in the process can be delicate. When situations are strained, professional organizers can mediate and create customized, win-win systems for everyone.

Ask Discovery Questions

Early in the assessment, we ask our clients, "Why do you want to get organized?" The answers to this question are actually the catalysts for change. If we can tune in to your reasons for wanting change, we can help you keep those catalysts in the front of your mind throughout the project. Often, the reasons you list for wanting to get organized will reflect your priorities and your points of pain.

Living among disorganization is painful. The next question we ask our clients taps into this pain: "What is your disorganization costing you?" It might be costing you late fees because you don't have a workable bill-paying system. You may be experiencing the pain of guilt because you are being wasteful with money by over-buying, replacing lost items, or just not planning ahead. Your pain can actually act as a powerful motivator to keep your organizing process going, so take the time to tune in to these negative outcomes of disorder. They will inspire you to forge ahead and reclaim your home. For more on the topic of how pain relates to the organizing process, visit *Reclaim Your Life,* chapter 8.

Closely related to the question of why you want to get organized is the next question we pose to our clients: What are your life priorities? We neglect or at least shortchange our true priorities when we are living out of control, disorganized lives. I invite you to think through what is truly important to you because your own life priorities are your most powerful motivators to reclaim your space and your life.

Examine the Job Description

Next, our organizers examine our client's job description. We want to know all the hats you're wearing, the roles you play, and your responsibilities at work, at home, and in extracurricular or volunteer capacities. As many of our clients begin to list their duties, they are surprised by their own scope of responsibilities. One reason people become disorganized is because they simply have too much on their plate. If this is a discovery you make about yourself, you must address your load to see lasting change.

If you are overloaded and overcommitted, your organizing efforts are unlikely to last. On the other hand, if you become aware of your overload and cut back, you can promote real change. Even customized, intuitive organizational systems will not last if they are not supported by good habits and maintenance. Sure, the overburdened mom can set up a good filing system, but if she is on four committees, volunteers at church, and is balancing three children and a part-time job, her filing system has virtually no chance to succeed because she is almost always absent from the home. In her hectic life she probably takes little or no time to process and file paper, so the filing system is unlikely to last without upkeep.

If you are taking on too much, now is the time to delegate to a spouse, children, or even hired professionals. To learn more about how to cut back your superfluous commitments, see *Reclaim Your Life,* chapter 10.

Assess Problem Areas

We want to help our clients celebrate what they are doing well, so we ask them what *is* working in their households. Once we know this, we can model after success. On the flip side, we also want to know what is *not* working. This gives clients the opportunity to brain dump their frustrations. From there, we can get more specific about their challenges with space, belongings, time, schedules, paper, habits, and any other personal issues. If you are serious about assessing the scope of your project, be sure to take the time to name your challenges in these specific areas.

As you can see, the intake assessment is more than a "get to know you" session. It can be exhausting and depressing for some people because they feel as if they are recounting their failures. Others can't stop talking because they feel relieved when they finally download to someone all the factors in their crazy lives that are contributing to their disorganization. I cannot recommend this assessment phase to you highly enough; if I could require it I would! I know that sounds strong, but without this foundation, your physical organizing work won't have any context, nor will you have articulated your reasons for and costs of disorder.

Space Tour

After the assessment, our organizers walk through the client's home room by room taking notes about what is going on in each space and how the client would like to use it. This process leads to a host of other discoveries, and the scope of the project comes into view. This is an essential step that requires the ability to step back and be objective about your space, which is hard to do precisely because it is *your* space! Having someone else act as tour guide during the intake assessment and space tour is incredibly useful when self-assessment is difficult. I've dedicated a whole chapter to conducting a space tour and the kinds of things you should look for in *Reclaim Your Life*, chapter 13.

I've been seeing Marisa now for six years. She has practically become family. However, the relationship didn't start that way! At her intake assessment, I could tell she was surprised by my seemingly endless string of questions. She got a little impatient during the process and asked, "When are we going to *organize?*" I could tell she thought the assessment was a waste of time, but I pressed on anyway.

At the end, I asked for a tour of the home, which she hurriedly gave me. Even though it was fast, I was able to do the necessary information-gathering. I tried to convince Marisa that her investment of time in these two steps was essential to the process and would pay off in time.

Marisa trusted me, and we dove into her home one room at a time. We are now in the maintenance stage, which some clients choose to manage on their own. Marisa, however, likes having me there once a month to help her comanage all the systems we set up together. My intimate knowledge of her life—thanks in large part to that assessment six years ago—helped us set up systems that still make perfect sense to her. We've been able to tweak her systems as her life and activities have evolved, but her core systems are still working. On many occasions Marisa has laughingly told me, "I thought you were crazy interviewing me like that, but now I'm so glad you did; just look at the years of benefit I've received from it." I encourage you to take Marisa's lead and embrace these two essential discovery steps *before* you take the plunge into the physical work of organizing.

Take the Plunge

You are probably anxious to dive into your sea of disorder and begin the process of sorting and purging, but first I'd like to share with you some of my philosophies that will sustain you for the long haul. I want you to take the plunge, but I also want you to know a little bit about the waters into which you will be diving!

We talked about the fact that being disorganized can be painful, but the organizing process can be painful as well. A true self-discovery process will stretch you. If you really want to know how you got where you are, you may come face-to-face with some self-defeating habits, shortcutting methods, and lifestyle choices. You could easily back out of the true organizing process and settle for tidying. Don't give up—the cost of that decision will keep you trapped in self-defeating behavior in the long run. If you can stare down and deal with your issues, you can break through to sustainable change. Remember, an authentic organizing process is far better than the counterfeit.

Go the Distance

Have you ever started an organizing project with great enthusiasm and then lost direction or momentum and abandoned it midway? I am in homes all the time that showcase half-finished projects. We all know where the road of good intentions leads, but sometimes we just get derailed. "Going the distance" is one of my key organizing philosophies. This means that once you invest in the process, you should commit to see your project all the way through if you want to see lasting change.

Total Burn Down

You must deal with every single item in the room or project you are tackling, leaving nothing unturned. You'll be tempted to deal with only *some* of the stuff or paper and push the rest aside for later. We often do this because we simply don't know what to do with the items or papers that are in our hands, so we set them down. When we do this over and over again, we are simply delaying resolution and perpetuating the problem.

I recommend that you force yourself to deal with every item or paper in the space in which you are working. Proceeding this way takes time, but it is thorough. When you do this and get to the bottom of the barrel, you will have accomplished what I call a total burn down. You will enjoy feeling free when you have dealt with everything, not allowing excuses and indecision to hijack your efforts. After a total burn down, you will finally feel in control of the situation because you will have total knowledge of the contents of the space. Getting through your items will take a while, but no more unknowns will be lurking in dark corners. For more on how to go the distance and achieve a total burn down, see *Reclaim Your Life*, chapter 12.

Ditch the Deadwood

In the process of dealing with backlog, you will find items you need to eliminate. I use the gardening metaphor of pruning to help people understand this important process of elimination and refinement. Deadwood is comprised of those items and papers that are no longer necessary, that are outdated, broken, or otherwise useless. Just as you will restore life to a plant when you extricate dead, broken, or clogging elements, your environment and time will breathe again when you prune.

You've probably heard that you should toss, purge, and recycle. Those terms are overused and little understood. They are just activities. Pruning, however, happens for a reason. We prune living things so that they can flourish; we are restoring circulation and vitality when we prune. Apply this gardening principle to your life, and you will begin to experience its benefits. To learn more about the spiritual nature of the Pruning Principle™, visit *Reclaim Your Life,* chapter 10.

Purpose Your Space

You're on a roll: You've committed to going the distance, you're burning down one room at a time, and you're pruning as you go. The next step is to determine how you will use your space. You've probably heard that items should have a "home" within your household so that you can put them away properly. I try to use this concept lightly, since many people (including me!) don't know what it really means. If you could find a home for something, wouldn't you have already done so? And what *doesn't* "finding a home" mean? Sure, I could find some coupons a home in the junk drawer, but that isn't really organizing, is it?

Because "finding a home" can be too open-ended, I've initiated the concept of "purposing" your space. In order to purpose your space, which I will refer to frequently in this book, you will need to think through the intended activity or purpose of each room or area. Sometimes a space can have limited multiple purposes, like a spare room that is both a home office and a craft room. Once you thoughtfully and intentionally purpose a space, you can empty the space of unrelated contents and put back only the materials and supplies that serve the intended purpose. As you do so, you may need to acquire more appropriate furniture or storage to accommodate these new purposes. In the case of the spare room, when you find nomadic arts and crafts items or office supplies elsewhere in the home, you will know the destination for those items.

Do What You Know First

As you progress in your organizing journey, your momentum will inspire you to keep going. Whenever you face indecision or frustration, just slow down and evaluate the situation. Some people experience this from the very beginning! They are so overwhelmed, they don't know where to begin. My advice to them is to simply ignore the unknown for a moment and do what you know first.

Pretend you are holding in your hands some insurance papers and some bank statements during your paper-sorting process. The bank statements seem obvious to you, and you are able to group them in the sorting process with other banking materials. Now you are left with the insurance papers, and you're not quite sure what to do with them. You don't know if they are financial papers or household papers. You are tempted just to set them down and move on to the next pile. Instead, grab a box and label it Unknown. Put the insurance papers into a temporary file and label it Homeowners or Auto Insurance or whatever makes the most sense to you. Set the file in the box.

When your filing system is completed you can return to the Unknown box to redistribute its contents. By then, you may have created a subsection under the financial category called Expenses into which the insurance papers might align perfectly. When you hold off on what you do *not* know and pursue what you *do* know, what you know begins to grow, and what you don't know begins to shrink.

Every organizing project I have ever tackled has proved this really does work! Try it for yourself when you get stuck!

If you engage in a discovery process that includes discovery-based conversation and touring the home, you are setting the foundation for long-term change. You will gain self-awareness and more commitment through your discoveries. Continue to apply discovery strategies, even as you take the plunge and dig in to the physical process. Remember, authentic organizing is as much about mind-set as it is about makeover!

You may have hoped that this chapter would give you a turnkey solution for every room of your home, but that's just not the way organizing works. No secret formula works for every person in every room. True organizing is a personalized, deductive process in which you gain self-awareness and momentum as you go. Yet if you can apply these assessment, space tour, and process strategies, you will have acquired more than a formula. You'll tap into a methodology that really works!

3

Customize Your Approach

I've SEEN A LOT OF PEOPLE FALL OFF the organizing wagon because they simply went too fast or too slow. Move through your projects at your natural pace and in the best work style for you. If you set out at a frantic pace and wildly start tossing and purging, you may quickly give up when you realize you are, in fact, on a long-term journey. On the other hand, if you just pick at the problem infrequently, you may find that your motivation and momentum disappear.

Likewise, some people try to impose solutions on themselves as if they are punishing themselves for bad behavior. They hope the imposed solution will whip them into shape. My observation is that the only solutions that work are the ones that are uniquely discovered for you. Imposed solutions just don't last. Discovered solutions, on the other hand, are built around your unique style, habits, lifestyle, and pace, so they make intuitive sense to you. These solutions are easier to maintain because you don't have to think so hard about what you were supposed to be doing. Instead, you can relax when you discover solutions that fit you!

Work with Your Natural Style

You'll see great success in your organizing journey when you begin to work with and not against yourself. So often, we read something in a magazine and try to force fit it onto our environment. We think that we have to organize in a certain way if we are going to get it right. On the contrary, organizing is all about working with your natural style and habits.

Teaming Up or Working Alone

When people hire my company, they've decided to partner with someone who can guide them through the organizing process. They've tried to solve their problems on their own, and it hasn't turned out as they had hoped. I encourage you to figure out whether your style is to partner or work on your own. Working with another person like an organizing consultant or a capable, committed friend might be a good fit for you if you need the guidance and accountability in your organizing journey. Others find that working alone can be an introspective, therapeutic experience. Others do both, working with an organizer and then working on their own between appointments as well. No approach is right or wrong; choose what works for you.

Working with Habits

If people in your family kick off their shoes when they enter the house, the likely result is a dangerous, spreading pile of shoes by the door that blocks traffic. To remedy this organizational clog, you can either *change* your habits or create a system to *manage* your habits. You could have family members take their shoes to their respective closets. On the other hand, you can adapt to the natural flow of things and put a basket or bin inside the door to capture shoes. A good organizing process is built around knowing which habits you will be willing to change and which you won't.

If your family is simply not going to take their shoes to their closets, you may be disappointed as you continue to live with the pile. A fancy shoe bench in the hallway might seem like a good solution, but if the shoe bench will only hold eight pairs of shoes it will quickly overflow. In this case, as in most cases, the organizing product was not the answer. Perhaps the best solution for your family would be to place a huge basket by the door and have people dump their shoes into it until it gets full. At the point of overflow, you can call everyone to claim their shoes. A "claim it or lose it" policy can move people to action! Organizing solutions are as unique as each family's habits.

Ability to Maintain

Without a doubt, working moms have it hard. Usually they are trying to raise the children, run the household, and hold down a job. Add to that the fact that most of them also do the family finances, grocery shopping, cleaning, meal planning and preparation, and social coordinating. No wonder professional women report a real challenge with getting and staying organized.

If you are rarely home because of uncontrollable circumstances, you may have to recruit some professional services to help. These services run the gamut from cleaning to running errands to organizing to childcare to travel planning to lawn care. If you can't afford to pay for professional services, you might be able to find others in your situation with whom you can swap responsibilities. Of course, as we discussed in the previous chapter, you may need to cut back on your extraneous commitments and responsibilities as well.

The point is that if you are never home, you are not going to have the time to maintain your household order, even if you've taken the time to deal with backlog and set up good systems. If your ability to maintain systems is very limited and yet you long for order, you must make some sacrifices. Either you will have to delegate some things that don't necessarily require your involvement (like cleaning and yard work) so you can concentrate on maintaining the household function and order, or you will have to delegate certain aspects of running the home. You'd be rather irrational to spend a lot of money and energy establishing systems only to abandon them due to lack of time. My advice is to consider your tradeoffs carefully and then put yourself in charge of the systems that most require your input and brainpower, delegating the rest.

Choose an Approach

I took seven years to finalize three approaches to the organizing process that I will share with you now. As I share the evolution of my understanding of these organizing approaches, you can examine your own thinking and decide which tactic you will apply.

Early in my organizing career, I made appointments with clients one at a time. At the end of each appointment, I pulled out my calendar and made another appointment. Though clients were happy with the progress, they didn't know what to expect. From appointment to appointment, we just did what we could accomplish in the allotted time.

I realized that my clients needed to understand the scope of their projects so they knew about how long they would take and the commitment they would require. Otherwise, people might wonder why I didn't wave my magic wand and resolve their entire organizing project in the first two appointments!

You may not know what to expect of the organizing process or of yourself as you tackle your space. If you don't have a grasp of the scope of your project, I recommend you spend more time listing your specific challenges, as we discussed in chapter 2.

The Series™

Early on, I realized that the most successful clients were the ones who were willing to dedicate a healthy chunk of time to working on their projects. I began explaining to prospective clients that disorganization doesn't happen overnight and that we would need periodic visits to unravel their chaos. An immediate shift happened for those who were serious about getting organized. I had communicated that several visits would be necessary, so they understood that this was a process, not a magic cure. They also had to make an up-front commitment of time, which weeded out those who would have cancelled anyway, citing time conflicts.

We discovered that for many people, working on organizing projects a little at a time is a user-friendly approach. Most of us have busy lives and families and struggle to carve out time for organizing. The vast majority of our clients book appointments in periodic visits, which we now call The Series. At every visit in a Series, we make progress and then assign follow-up items to our clients that they can do on their own. Most people love this strategy because it is manageable, offers steady and sure progress, and saves them time and money.

How often is often enough to work on your home-organizing projects? Some people want to work on their projects every week. Others can only work once every two to three weeks because of time or budget constraints. We've found that the clients who get the most out of The Series are the ones who work once a week or every two weeks. One caution as you consider addressing your problem in installments: A month or more between organizing sessions is just too much time. Think about it. When you make a little headway but wait an entire month to resume your work on something, you lose momentum, desire, and commitment. You can apply what I've learned; set a weekly or biweekly schedule to begin your own organizing Series.

How long should each organizing session last? After you've established the frequency of your series schedule, you can try it a few times before you decide the optimal length of each working session. Have you ever noticed that when we watch a few shows on television or go out to eat, a few hours is gone in the blink of an eye? Yet we become miserly with our time when investing in our own quality of life! Older folks or those with attention issues may need shorter time blocks, and that's okay. Remember, good organizing is all about what works for you!

The Blitz™

For people who are chomping at the bit to conquer their mess as quickly as possible, the steady-and-sure Series may not seem appealing. Some people don't want installments of progress; they want to raze their home to the ground and start over! And they want it fast!

Back-to-back, longer sessions allow you to make more progress more quickly. Sometimes people call us and have a deadline for which they must prepare. For them, a Series would take too long. They want to compress their organizing sessions over a short period of time and prefer The Blitz.

What kind of people or situations call for a Blitz? People who have spring break off work might want to dedicate the entire week to restoring household order. Home-based business owners who experience a yearly slowdown during the holidays might want to organize their home office in a concentrated time frame. During the summer, lots of folks want to attack their garage or shed in a short period of time while the weather holds out.

Certain rooms, like garages and kitchens, are best done in a Blitz approach due to their frequency of use. To organize either of these spaces, you must get everything out where you can see it, categorize it, group it, and purge it. Then you need to clean out the space before you reintroduce order. You certainly wouldn't want to drag all your garage belongings out into the driveway, push the pause button, and then restart the project two weeks later. Once your stuff is in the driveway, you have to power through and keep going (especially if it rains)! Likewise, you don't want to be stepping over your kitchen dishes or pantry items as you work on your kitchen over a four-week period. Diving in and tackling either of these spaces all at once is much more efficient!

People who have been using a Series approach can switch to a Blitz approach if they want to take their progress to a new level. We call it a fast-forward. Let's say you have ten years of backlog in your home. You never moved in properly and set up good systems, and you've been adding insult to injury with your rapid accumulation. You've been working once a week for the last few months on your organizing projects, but you've been working alone. Progress has been steady and sure, but all you've finished is your home office and your bedroom. Now you want to get through the playroom and basement. Summer is coming up, and you'll have more time off. You can fast-forward your progress by scheduling several days in a row to aggressively address each of these spaces. A Blitz might be just what the doctor ordered to fast-forward your installment approach to the next level!

A Blitz isn't for everyone. People who can't dedicate several consecutive days to a project shouldn't try a Blitz. If you don't understand the scope of the project or aren't good at visualizing how to get from where you are now to the end result, you will want to think twice before scheduling a Blitz. You may get in over your head. Older folks who have limited mobility or energy also aren't good candidates for a Blitz. One of the nice things about a Series is that you have the ability to work more organically and methodically through your space. The Blitz requires faster decisions and is more intense work.

Nothing is magical about the time frame in which a Blitz is conducted. It could be an entire weekend of back-to-back days. It could be eight-hour days on Monday, Wednesday, and Friday, allowing you a breather in between. The key is that a Blitz provides dedicated, concentrated time to allow you to make major progress quickly. If working swiftly and intensely is more your style, schedule a customized Blitz for yourself today!

Group Therapy™

Finally, there are some projects that a Series or a Blitz can't touch with a ten-foot pole. When you need a serious intervention, it's time for Group Therapy! Projects of considerable scope sometimes require more than one person. I have established this offering for people who want to hire a team of people to tackle their project and are willing to dedicate the funds for many hired hands.

What kinds of people or situations call for Group Therapy? Excessive accumulation or huge undertakings make this approach a good choice. We recommend this attack when we encounter massive projects like packed households that are stacked to the rafters because of compulsive accumulation or household moves. A squad of people can quickly tackle situations like these using a Group Therapy approach.

We've found that sending in only one organizer to help a client with a project of enormous size can be ineffective and defeating for the client. You wouldn't send one soldier into battle to rescue a downed man; you would send in a rescue team. When a project drags on because it is simply more than two people can manage alone, the client begins to lose hope like a wounded soldier waiting interminably for rescue.

Think of Group Therapy as "manning up" a Blitz. Multiple people working toward the same goal creates synergy and forward momentum. A properly equipped team can swiftly and efficiently sweep through years of backlog.

Bear in mind that for true organizing to take place and your efforts to last during a team project, the decision maker (you!) will need to be involved every step of the way. Group Therapy is not a way to get other people to tackle your projects *for* you; it is a way to *manage* a massive project. You will still need a discovery process, an understanding of your individual needs and lifestyle, and a plan.

If the idea of Group Therapy appeals to you, you have two options. The first choice is to hire a group of professional organizers to guide and manage your project. The advantage of this tactic is that experts will get you from start to finish. You can rely on someone else to be project manager instead of having to figure out the plan and action steps yourself. You can take on the role of a decision maker whose opinions and desires are the priority. The trade-off with this option is that you will have to dedicate resources to invest in this personalized, concentrated assistance.

Another choice is to enlist family members, neighbors, or friends. The obvious advantage of this option is to save money. You will need to appoint a capable, responsible project manager who can see the big picture and the steps to achieve it. One trade-off with this option is that the project manager is often the same person as the decision maker, which can bog down effective execution. If you are both, you will have to deal with helpers coming to you with constant questions while you are juggling the project. Another thing to consider is that volunteer labor (especially family!) can be flaky and counterproductive to the process. On the up side, however, many people find a friends-and-family Group Therapy approach to be a bonding, fruitful experience that develops skills for all participants.

One caution with bringing in nonprofessionals for Group Therapy: Leave the paper to the experts! Garages, kitchens, basements, household moves, and even downsizing are all great projects for either professionals or an informal team. When it comes to paper, though, you don't want many pairs of hands touching your sensitive documents. You don't want important papers to get tossed or shredded without your approval. Since paper provides a record of your personal and professional life, you probably don't want just anyone sifting through it. Consider budgeting time and resources with an expert to effectively categorize and manage your documents.

I hope our experiences and approaches are instructive for you. Our methods remain the same in any project, but our approaches vary according to the client's needs, goals, and time frame. Choose the approach that best suits your lifestyle, and get ready to take back your life! If you work within your natural habits, pace, and work style, you'll find that you can achieve your own definition of organizing success!

Part Two

Public Spaces

Chapter 4: The Kitchen

Chapter 5: The Family Room

Chapter 6: The Living Room

Chapter 7: The Dining Room

Chapter 8: The Playroom

The public rooms of our homes include those into which we commonly invite outsiders. Anyone who has ever had a party knows that partygoers congregate in the kitchen. Teen guests gravitate toward the television and games in the family room. Play dates between toddlers might happen in the playroom. Public spaces must first serve the people living in the home; they must make sense for the way you actually live. As you establish purposes and order in each of these rooms, you will find that they will become more presentable and enjoyable for guests as well.

Hard-and-fast rules will not help you organize your home. Part 2 won't give you a detailed plan for each public space because your home is unique to you and your family. In these pages you will, however, find stories from the front lines of my work as a professional organizer and some successful room conversions that may inspire you. This part will offer you strategies to tackle the organizing process and some pitfalls to avoid in each space. Get ready to view and organize your home in a whole new way!

4
The Kitchen

W E SPEND MOST OF OUR WAKING HOURS in just a few rooms of our homes. I don't know about you, but other than sleeping in my bedroom, I spend the most time in my office and my kitchen. Fortunately for me, my office is adjacent to my kitchen, so while I'm working I have easy access to snacks!

When our organizers help clients with household moves, the kitchen takes the longest to pack and unpack. That's because so much stuff is crammed in the kitchen! This room probably has more drawers and cabinets than any other room in the home. From gadgets to appliances to utensils to dishes to food, hundreds—maybe thousands—of unique items must be stored and accessed.

In addition to storing a lot of items, the kitchen is usually buzzing with activity. The kitchen isn't just the mess hall; it's the center of the home. The daily mundane chores of our lives usually take place in the kitchen: washing our hands, getting the dog a treat, preparing and serving food, processing the mail. Kids often want to do their homework in the kitchen, and meanwhile their backpacks, permission slips, and schoolwork follow behind them. Craft projects that are too messy to do over the carpet end up spread out on the kitchen table. Briefcases and purses and wallets and keys land on the countertops. No wonder the kitchen is one of the most frustrating, messy spaces in the home. We spend the majority of our time here, so if it always looks like it was struck by a hurricane, the kitchen can become a depressing place to be!

With a huge volume of contents and many decisions to make, I recommend to all my clients that they take a threefold approach to kitchens. You will want to Blitz, customize, and phase your kitchen project to ensure long-term success.

Blitzing

As a professional organizer, I can assure you that kitchens should be organized in a two- to four-day Blitz. Kitchens are like garages; you can't empty their contents, leave everything spread out for weeks on end, and expect to continue to function normally. Overhauling the kitchen will take some serious effort in a compressed period of time.

If you are ready to tackle the kitchen, be prepared to invest 16 to 32 hours, depending on the amount of disorganization and whether you are including the pantry in the project. I guarantee you this: A piecemeal kitchen organization project will make you hate yourself and your kitchen. If you schedule a three-day Blitz, however, you will have dedicated enough time and will have given yourself permission to spread out temporarily, all with an end in sight.

Customizing

I could write an entire book on organizing your kitchen, and perhaps someday I will do just that. For now, however, I have only one chapter to share with you my insider's secrets to a well-ordered kitchen. Your kitchen should reflect your priorities and your lifestyle. To create and sustain order in your kitchen, you will need to evaluate the kind of person you are and determine how to set up your kitchen around your unique interests and needs.

One of my favorite clients is Roseann. She absolutely loves to cook. She enjoys quality wine, delicious food, and fine living. Her kitchen, however, was not a reflection of her culinary passions. She was tired of digging in cabinets for the right dish or pan. She bought things that disappeared into her cabinets, never to be used and enjoyed. She was ready to make her kitchen serve her needs and avoid the daily frustration of a kitchen that didn't work for her.

Our primary challenge was that Roseann is only five feet tall and can't reach very high without a stool. Even though she had a lot of storage, much of it wasn't all that useful for someone of her stature. Things were stored where they fit and not where they made the most sense or where they were the most accessible, which left her climbing like a monkey around her kitchen to retrieve even the most basic items.

I wanted to set up her kitchen in a manner that put her most frequently used items at her fingertips—underneath the countertop or in the bottom shelf of the upper cabinets. That meant that we had to evaluate each item we found on the basis of how regularly she used it. With this goal, we dove into her project determined to make this space work for our petite chef.

Phasing

If you attempt to take on a massive project like a kitchen in one fell swoop, you may quickly find yourself in over your head. For this reason, I suggest that you divide your project days into phases, working at accomplishing only one thing at a time. Once you've completed one step, you can move on to the next. If you try to empty, sort, make decisions, and reload cabinets all at once, you will likely become confused and distracted, and your kitchen organization project will become a never-ending story.

Phase 1: Total Burn Down

Applying the total burn down (which we discussed in chapter 2), we emptied the entire kitchen, leaving no quiche pan unturned. Roseann was surprised by how long this process took, even though I had brought another organizer with me to expedite the project. We carried each delicate glass and serving piece into the dining room and carefully set it on the table. (We put all the leaves in the table for this purpose.) We reunited all the cookbooks in a big box, collected every plastic storage container and lid into a series of boxes, and even grouped the food from her pantry by type. By the end of the first eight-hour day, the three of us had emptied her entire kitchen and wiped down her cabinets. Three rooms of the main floor were covered with boxes, baskets, and piles of kitchen gear. Phase 1 was complete.

Phase 2: Pruning

The next morning, we returned fresh and began phase 2. We went through each box and made decisions. We applied the Pruning Principle (see chapter 10 of *Reclaim Your Life*) and eliminated the superfluous belongings that were taking up room and energy.

When we had assembled all her travel coffee mugs into one box, Roseann was shocked to see that she had 19 mugs for a family of four! She quickly pawed through the box and pitched 12 mugs, keeping only the ones that were in the best shape. Her plastic storage ware was next on our list. Roseann took special delight in eliminating the old, stained containers. In the process, she found many lids without containers and containers without lids. She wondered out loud why in the world she had kept such mismatched items and had continued to accumulate more and more.

She said she was learning a lot about her own habits by going through this process. Life moves so fast that we often keep things we've always used, not because we should but because keeping something and moving on is easier than stopping and making a decision. By the end of six hours, we had sorted through all the boxes, started piles of items to donate, and thinned out all the boxes that remained. We had ditched the deadwood in her kitchen, and phase 2 was complete.

Phase 3: Assessing Available Storage

Once we knew how much of each type of item Roseann wanted to keep, we had a better idea of how much space she needed to accommodate each category. In the remaining two hours of our eight-hour day, we sketched out the cabinets and took a hard look at the available real estate in her kitchen. In phase 3 we created centers and identified the most frequently used items.

Creating centers is not a hard science; it is a give-and-take process because keeping like items together must be balanced by how frequently something is used.

Every kitchen needs a food preparation center near the sink where mixing bowls, knives, measuring cups, cutting boards, and the like can be stored for easy access. Pots, pans, and oven-safe dishes should live in a cooking center along with spoons and spatulas. In Roseann's kitchen, we identified a food storage center (since this was used daily, we wanted it easily accessible in pull-out drawers) and a serving center for platters (less often used, so we located it over the fridge) based on which cabinets were available and how frequently she used the contents. Our centers helped us to "purpose" Roseann's cabinets for specific uses (for more on how to "purpose" your space, see chapter 14 in *Reclaim Your Life*).

Before filling the cabinets back up with their new contents, we marked each cabinet with a Post-it note with its intended items like "storage ware" or "everyday dishes" to indicate our intentions for that space. Then we stepped away from our organizing process momentarily and went shopping.

Phase 4: Applying Products

There is a difference between accumulating storage products and applying them. We wait to shop until we know everything we can possibly know about the client's belongings that need to be stored. I want to know the quantity and measurements of the items. Carefully applying the right product at the right time in the process will save you a lot of money and frustration in the long run.

During our project, I discovered that Roseann had a habit of collecting water bottles. Much like her travel mugs, her water bottles had multiplied like rabbits. In our process, we found 20 water bottles, which she reduced to eight. By using a fixed-sized bin to store the ones she decided to keep, we were able to fend off her collecting habits. This way, if she did add more, she would have to follow the "one in, one out" rule and part with an older one to make room for the new one. Using containers to group and store your items is a wonderful way to limit the growth of that particular category. Roseann was enthusiastic about this proposition, wanting to do everything she could to maintain the precious state of order she was working so hard to achieve. When we were at the store, we purchased a bin that fit the eight water bottles perfectly.

Roseann was going to store her serving pieces in her kitchen above the fridge, and she wanted easy access to them. Yet serving dishes are usually large and heavy and stacking them in a high place creates a problem because you have to get on a stool to reach them, and then lift a heavy stack of dishes to pull out one item, putting yourself and your dishes at risk. We determined that Roseann had ten platters and serving pieces altogether, so we purchased two five-sectioned dish separators to stand her serving pieces vertically on their side. We had measured each cabinet, so we knew that two of these five-sectioned separators would fit in this space.

Roseann and I took another two hours to list and purchase the products we needed for her kitchen. Our eight-hour work day had turned into a ten-hour day, but we both knew the time was well spent. All this measuring and figuring out what products you need may sound like a waste of time. But a storage product is only a *solution* if it solves a problem and makes your life easier. If you buy products prematurely in the organizing project, you are likely to have accumulated plastic without applying a solution.

Phase 5: Reloading

Roseann and I were 18 hours into her project when I returned on the third workday. We had scheduled a six-hour day for this process. Day three sped by as everything just fell into place. Our work and storage centers materialized beautifully as we loaded the intended items into their clearly marked locations. If you roll out a project in phases, the closer you get to the end, the more momentum you pick up.

Before we began our project, Roseann had a small counter space piled high with cookbooks and paper. Below it lived a junk drawer and some pull-out shelves, and above the counter were glass-faced doors with random appliances and bowls stuck inside where they fit. We had not quite known what to do with this space as we were assessing her available storage. (Often, you just have to do what you know first, and what you don't know will resolve itself with time.) As the rest of her cabinets were being reloaded and more and more centers were created, we began to close in on her project. Suddenly, a delicious idea occurred to me, and I asked her to focus her attention on the pantry while I worked on this odd little space.

An hour later, I had created a little bar for this wine aficionada. I arranged the counter with a tray and some wine bottles. I filled the drawer with corkscrews and other wine accoutrements. In the pull-out drawers I stacked her wine on its side. In the glass cabinets above the counter I carefully arranged all her wine glasses by size, with her favorites on the lowest shelves. When I revealed this area to Roseann, she squealed in delight. By doing what we knew first, we had truly customized this space to her tastes.

After 24 hours of work, Roseann had a kitchen that she could not wait to unveil to the world. She rattled on about how excited she was that the holidays were coming and chatted about all the baking and cooking she was planning. Her eyes sparkled as she opened each cabinet and admired our handiwork. By Blitzing, customizing, and phasing, we had accomplished our goal of creating a Roseann-friendly kitchen that she could share with loved ones.

A lot of people get gun-shy when they hear that a kitchen really can take this long to properly organize. They think they don't have the time to take on a project of this scope, yet every day they live with wasted time and energy, which quickly add up to days and days of fruitless effort. They think they will shortcut the process, yet when they do they are faced with growing confusion and a bigger mess. Take it from me; I've seen hundreds of kitchen projects. If I knew of a quicker way to properly establish a kitchen, I would tell you! I want your kitchen, a room that you spend many of your waking hours inside, to literally purr for you.

Hot Spots

My space is running out in this chapter to share kitchen advice with you, so let's review worst kitchen hot spots and some of my favorite kitchen organizing strategies.

Accumulation

- Avoid multiplying coffee mugs, water bottles, and plastic storage ware. Limit yourself by containing each of these categories into a drawer or bin.

- Ditch your extra plastic and paper bags. They block up drawers and cabinets and rob you of storage space. If you keep some, have a reason and a purpose. I use my plastic grocery bags to line wastebaskets and to take on walks with my dog.

- Resist reusing plastic tubs, such as butter containers. People like to reuse containers, but you can't see into them, and the plastic will eventually give off chemicals. Instead, use the store-bought kind that are created for this purpose and congratulate yourself for recycling the others.

General Storage

- If you have a dining room or even a hutch, try to consolidate your china, crystal, and formal serving pieces here rather than hogging kitchen space for these items.

- Take advantage of vertical space like tall cabinets by installing an additional shelf or using shelf dividers and dish separators to create more storage.

- If you tend to lose or forget about stowed items that you cannot see, invest in converting some of your lower fixed shelves into pull-out shelves.

Food Storage

- Just as you created centers in your kitchen, create centers for categories of items in your pantry. In my pantry, I have shelves for snacks, breakfast, baking, dinner, and paper goods and containers. Each shelf is labeled, and I store items of like type in smaller containers for easy removal and use.

- Gut your refrigerator regularly. Use what you have before you buy more, and shop with a list.

- Chop up healthy foods like veggies and cheese into bite-sized pieces and leave them in containers in the fridge to make nutritious eating easy.

Paper

- Deal with the mail daily. Most families I've met process incoming mail in the kitchen. Without vigilant sorting, shredding, and processing, piles will grow sky-high fast. Keep a garbage can, recycle bin, and shredder nearby.

- If you don't have a home office, establish one so you can send completed paperwork to it for permanent storage.

Otherwise, the kitchen may become the final resting place for paper of all descriptions.

- Immediately create a household hub (see the next section in this chapter) to help you manage paper and tasks that inevitably land in the kitchen.

Kid-Friendly Kitchens

- Accept the fact that young children will gravitate to the kitchen. Establish a play drawer just for them. Fill it with plastic storage containers and lids that don't match, old linens, or anything creative to stimulate their imagination.

- If your kids like to do their homework in the kitchen, establish boundaries for what they can and can't use on or near the table. It can be a useful work or play surface without becoming a storage surface!

- As your kids age, help them to contribute to chores by storing dishes low enough that they can help set the table, wash dishes, and unload the dishwasher.

- Store healthy snacks, juice boxes, and lunch fixings on a low shelf so kids can help make their own lunches.

- Until your kids reach a reasonable age (and only you know what that is), keep caffeinated and sugared foods under *your* control so you can keep kids under control!

The Household Hub

I cannot end this all-important chapter without giving you a way to fend off the tidal wave of paper and family belongings that assault the kitchen on a daily basis. If you cannot remember what laminate covers your counters because they are layered with paper, art projects, purses, and clutter, you will need to overhaul your kitchen *and* create a household hub.

Every kitchen can use a miniature business center because much of life's business is transacted in this bustling area. Think of it as your household command center. Some kitchens come equipped with a small desk with drawers and even upper cabinets, creating an ideal spot for the hub. In other kitchens, our organizers have to get more creative, dedicating a few feet of counter space, a drawer or two, and a set of cabinets to this purpose.

Each hub will look a little different from household to household. Yet we see some recurring needs in every home. You can set up a phone center in your hub for your phone, notepaper, and pens so you can take messages. Many hubs include a chalkboard, whiteboard, or bulletin board on the wall to capture messages. (I prefer chalk or white boards because a corkboard can attract all kinds of other clutter). This board can also double as a family communication center where kids and adults can leave notes to each other.

The hub is also your mail room, where you process the mail and queue it for action. It is your first line of defense. A good hub should have a garbage bin, recycle bin, and shredder nearby so you can get rid of the junk mail and credit card offers safely. Hubs need an office-supply drawer, complete with a three-hole punch, a stapler, a letter opener, pens, pencils, highlighters, paper clips, and the like. The more paper and bills you can quickly process here, the more easily you can transfer them to your home office seamlessly. Many of our clients store their reference books here, including cookbooks, dictionary and thesaurus, and phone directories.

Since each hub is customized to its users, your drawers and cabinets might store things your neighbor's hub will not. Our organizers will often include in the hub a modest utility drawer with a hammer, picture hooks, nails, matches, batteries, a tape measure, and other frequently used items because families are always reaching for these items. Someone with a nearby mudroom or utility room, however, may not need a utility drawer in their hub. Some people like to store their camera, film, and video camera in the hub if they have enough space. Many of our clients also like to set up a craft drawer or two for the kids if they do their projects at the kitchen table or at the hub itself.

If room is available, we will often include a desktop or laptop computer at the hub. Having a computer nearby is helpful for managing the family calendar, handling e-mail, finding recipes and directions online, and checking the weather. A computer-equipped hub can double as a homework center for the kids while providing much-needed computer supervision in a public space.

Hands-down, however, our clients' favorite tool of the household hub is definitely the Restoring Order Household Reference Binder™ that we set up for almost all our clients. This binder stores your take-out menus, coupons, gift certificates, bus routes, team rosters, sports and school schedules, emergency contacts, membership information, and more. The paper that is currently taped inside your cabinets, stuck on your fridge, shoved in the junk drawers, and lying around your kitchen is probably there for a reason. This is paper you look at a lot, like the menu for the local pizza joint, so it just hangs out until it's used. I call this "perpetual" paper because it stays around perpetually until you get a new menu, join a new Bunko group, or send your kids to a new school. Corralling all this frequently referenced paper into one binder provides household managers with a powerful tool to juggle the family's activities. You can make your own household reference binder or find our customizable binder on our website at www.RestoringOrder.com.

5

The Family Room

THE FAMILY ROOM IS THE GATHERING PLACE in most homes. It's the room in which we throw baby showers, eat popcorn in front of the television, and play games with the kids. In some homes, the family room is also known as the great room or the recreation room. Unlike its dusty, neglected counterpart, the living room, the family room is typically a high-traffic, high-energy room.

Location, Location, Location

I grew up in a home built in the 1950s, and our family room was a spacious, independent room in the basement. Most days, it was cool and dark, and it didn't get much use. However, when our friends came over to play, it was the room where they joined my brother and me as we played charades, built forts, and jumped from couch to couch. Delightfully, it was far removed from our parents, so we could make a lot of noise.

Independent Room

Our basement family room was also our Christmas room. Its best feature was the wood-burning fireplace. Our family room glowed with a popping, crackling fire every Christmas. We hung our stockings on the mantle and tacked the greeting cards to the wall. Our presents were stockpiled and opened here as we gathered in our pajamas every Christmas morn.

If your family room is in another part of the house as was mine, you can define how and when you use the room. You might use it for holidays the way we did. You can banish the noisy kids to this room when you've had enough. You may even decide that it is the domain of a specific person or activity, like a husband's card playing room or the wife's scrapbook station. The point is this: An independent room gives you options because of its location. If it is in a highly trafficked area, it might be used a lot by every member of the household and host a multitude of activities. In that case, see some of my suggestions in the next section for corralling clutter and establishing rules. If your family room is in a more remote part of the home, you may have to make more of an effort to identify its purpose and use it.

Here are some questions you can ask yourself if you are using an independent room as a family room:

- If it rarely gets used, why? Have your kids outgrown it? Is it acting more like a storage room than a family room? Getting to the root of the problem will help you revitalize this space.

- If you aren't using the family room as often as you'd like, can you convert its purpose to something more useful?

- Is it for entertaining guests or for family use only?

- Are your kids old enough to be unsupervised in this room?

A Room Adjoining the Kitchen

Many newer homes feature a family room that is adjacent to the kitchen in an open, accessible location. Since the kitchen is the axis of family life, an adjoining family room becomes a comfortable extension of the kitchen and joins in the bustle of activity. This room is often dubbed the great room since it expands the kitchen in length and serves many purposes.

Personally, I think a family room that is adjacent to the kitchen is ideal. Most likely, if you have a space like this, your family will congregate in this area more often than any other space in the home. If you are looking to establish a household nucleus, create a kitchen-family room combination.

Family rooms that connect to the kitchen have high traffic. Try to use the same sturdy flooring in both rooms. This allows for maximum wear and the most flexibility of furniture arrangement. If you can afford to choose new flooring to give the rooms a conjoined appearance, choose a floor that's easy to clean and won't show a lot of stains.

Because the family room is usually filled with people, you will want to prevent the creeping clutter that comes with more traffic by defining the purposes this room will serve. For example, if you decide that this room will serve as the entertainment center of the household, all music, videos, and games can be located here. In order to make room for those things, you will need to eliminate things that do not serve the entertainment purpose. That seems simple enough, but many family rooms are clogged up with paper piles, backpacks, pet supplies, books, and basically anything that was dropped along the traffic trail. Depositing nomadic items in the family room is a common bad habit.

If you struggle with a family room that is layered with items that don't belong, create a Go Elsewhere basket that nomadic items can be loaded into and relocated at the end of every evening. This daily distribution can be one of the children's chores, teaching them to put things where they belong. Alternatively, family members could have their own basket or bin in this room to capture their traveling treasures, and they could be responsible to empty it daily. Confiscating kids' items from overflowing, neglected baskets can be an effective teaching technique!

The family room is where people spend a lot of their time, so bad habits will surface quickly here. Snacking and eating meals in front of the television is easy when the food is close at hand! Nothing is inherently wrong with eating in front of the television; my husband, Trevor, and I eat on television trays quite frequently. The problem occurs when sauce, juice, and grease begin to show up on your upholstery or floor or when the dog is better fed between the cushions than from his own bowl. All too often pop cans and bags of Cheetos are left on the coffee table for mom to clean up. Catch my drift? If you are going to allow your family to treat the family room like an extended dining room, it will become messy quickly unless you establish some simple rules of etiquette and self-management.

Points to consider if you have adjoining spaces:

- High-traffic family rooms that adjoin the kitchen will benefit from sturdy, easy-to-clean flooring.

- Creeping clutter can be kept at bay by defining the purpose of the family room and locating only the related equipment and supplies in the room, eliminating unrelated items.

- Using a general or individualized Go Elsewhere basket system will help keep this room clear and teach valuable accountability skills.

- Rules surrounding food consumption and cleanup will prevent your family room from becoming disorganized and dirty.

Activities and Storage

As I mentioned above, the best way to organize your family room and ensure that it stays orderly is to define its purpose. To learn more about consolidating activities and supplies together in specific areas of your home, see chapter 14 of *Reclaim Your Life*.

The most common uses of family rooms I've seen are watching television and videos, playing games (both traditional and electronic), listening to music, gathering socially, and reading. You'll want to store the items that serve these activities nearby. The nature and quantity of what you will store depends on your interests and habits.

Television typically dominates most family rooms, so the all-important remote is usually assigned a place of honor on the coffee table or end table. If your family watches videos in the family room, find appropriate storage for VHS tapes and DVDs. (Some of my more technically savvy clients download their movies and store them in an electronic format so they have less to physically store.) If you use them here, games and puzzles also need to find a destination in the family room. If you read books and peruse magazines in your family room, you'll need appropriate shelf space or containers. Since all these entertainment activities often converge in one room, you'll need adequate storage that suits your belongings.

Furniture Choices

Joanie had all the wrong furniture in her family room. She had two couches that she had placed corner to corner at a 90-degree angle with a coffee table in the middle. This arrangement works well in many rooms, but in Joanie's compact family room, family members had to climb on top of one couch to reach the other. Piles of blankets and pillows sat on the couches along with empty bags of chips and the family dog. One of the couches was also a fold-out bed, but it never got used because of poor access.

Lest you think that Joanie was the only one to blame for the family room disorder, her husband and sons added fuel to the dis-organization fire. An armoire held the TV and was exploding with entertainment options. Videos stood three rows deep on the armoire shelves, so when Joanie's husband wanted to watch *Braveheart,* he emptied the movies onto the floor to sort through them. He left the wreckage from his search on the floor or haphazardly shoved it back into any available space.

Joanie's teenage sons had plugged all their video game joysticks into the equipment inside the cabinet, and the controls and cords were strewn on the floor in front of the television, tripping passersby. Her sons didn't replace the games in their cases when they were done, so scores of unmatched games and cases littered the area. The movies took up the only storage space the armoire offered, so the video games never got put away. As a result, the separated games and cases were shoved in every nook and cranny of the armoire. Some of the boy's favorite card games and music CDs sat atop the stereo in the armoire. Their board games were strewn throughout the house, and a few recently played games were shoved against the family room wall.

In order for Joanie's family to restore order to the family room, they had to work on picking up after themselves and putting things away. However, their habits were bad in part because their storage was inadequate. If the boys didn't have enough room to properly house the games, they had no incentive to reassemble games with cases and put them where they belong. One root cause of disorganization is inappropriate or insufficient storage for the type and quantity of items you need to store. Joanie's family had this problem.

Joanie needed to evaluate what was really going on. Sometimes people beat themselves up for being slobs when in reality their problem is partially due to their furniture choices. When I sat down with Joanie to review the situation in her family room, I learned that she didn't even have a VHS player anymore. It broke, and she gave it away. I asked her why she was keeping all the VHS video tapes, and she said she hadn't got around to pitching them when she eliminated the video player, and then she forgot about it. I suggested that a local library would be happy to have the VHS tapes, so we loaded all of them into a few bags that she could deliver to the library.

Among the DVDs that remained, we discovered at least a dozen movies that her sons had outgrown, so those went into the library bags as well. She commented sheepishly that she didn't know why she was holding onto those movies and added that they were stuck at the back of the layered rows of videos. We lined up her leftover

DVDs on the floor to assess how much shelf space she would need to store them one layer deep. We determined that she would need at least four three-foot shelves for this purpose.

We gathered the nomadic games throughout the house into the family room. Some had been stashed in the coat closet downstairs, some lived in the boys' bedrooms, and others were lurking in the linen closet upstairs. Once we could see all the games, Joanie separated out the games her family didn't use or had outgrown, and we bagged those up for charity. We stacked the remaining games in three piles by size so we could evaluate quantity. We determined that she needed at least three shelves to keep all the games together and allow a little room for growth.

We found only a few CDs at the back of the armoire even though the unit contained a stereo. I asked Joanie where the rest of the CDs were, and she pointed to her master bedroom, where she and her husband liked to listen to music. Her sons now had iPods and downloaded all their music online, so their CDs had gradually disappeared. The family rarely used the stereo in the armoire anymore, so we disconnected it and moved it to the bedroom, replacing the older model that lived there.

As we were emptying the armoire we found most of the boys' lost video games and cases. We matched them up and found about 40 games of different sizes and descriptions. We wound up all the cords around the joysticks and controls, and we started another pile of video equipment. In all, we decided that we would need two large drawers to store this odd-sized, ever-changing technology.

In our discovery process, Joanie and I learned how her family *actually* used their entertainment equipment and materials. We were able to eliminate both hardware and software because of our discoveries. Joanie and I looked at some furniture catalogs, and we went online to look at armoire options. Before long, we identified a large armoire unit with bifold doors, multiple adjustable-height shelves, and two drawers that would work much better for the items Joanie's family uses. As we were purchasing it, we noticed a matching chest-style coffee table, and I encouraged Joanie to replace her dated glass-top coffee table with this piece so she could store her blankets and pillows. She was delighted and ordered the items.

I don't want you to get the impression that you always have to buy things to properly organize. Remember, restoring order is not just about buying products; it's about introducing the right product at the right time in the process. If Joanie had very limited funds but some time to look, we could have found secondhand items online or at garage sales. If Joanie chose not to upgrade her furniture, I would have searched around her house for an unused bookshelf, hauled it into the family room, and identified it as the new home of DVDs and games. (I've done this many times for families.) If she didn't have a spare bookshelf, we could have at least loaded each type of item into a separate bin to store on the floor (clearly labeled, of course) until she could save up for a more appropriate storage unit. Organizing isn't about shelling out money for fancy furniture; you can find many modest solutions if you look around. However, saving for and investing in proper storage is important if you want to save yourself daily headaches and eliminate exploding clutter.

Season of Life

I hope you're seeing that organizing your family room is about so much more than finding a home for things. It begins with knowing the purpose and use of the room and will include evaluating the location, activities, necessary storage, and available furniture. Now add to all of these considerations the trump card of the family room: The season of life you're in really helps shape and define the use of your family room.

If you're living the bachelor life, your iPod might be your pride and joy. Downloading and storing your music by genre or artist might be your favorite activity. Investing in adjustable lighting and matching furniture might be your priority.

If you don't have children adding to the chaos in your family room, you will likely have different needs and supplies in this room. If you entertain friends and throw parties in the space, you will place a lower priority on visual entertainment and a higher priority on experiential entertainment.

When small children are afoot, you might find yourself looking for ways to hide huge plastic toys behind the couch. Your priority might be to disguise the floor stains with throw rugs and keep sharp things out of reach. Educational videos might be a staple in your daily routine, so keeping those accessible is paramount to the parent whose toddler is begging for Cookie Monster's song or a specific Veggie Tales story.

Teens and their friends, interests, and eating habits eventually impose themselves on family rooms. Determining which kinds of activities actually take place in this room is vital. Why take up valuable shelf space with books and magazines if no one reads in here and frequently used games and videos are shoved in drawers and sitting on the floor? After identifying how you will use the space, establishing rules for food consumption and cleanup just might save your sanity.

Knowing how each family uses its family room is impossible without actually visiting the home and engaging in a discovery process. Remember my old family room? It was moderately used when we were kids, but only for specific purposes. Its uses and the things we stored inside were unique to our family. It didn't require a lot of thought or upkeep. Other family rooms, like Joanie's, are heavily used, highly trafficked spaces that require not only appropriate storage but also ongoing evaluation and pruning. Whether you have an independent or conjoined family room, whether it is quiet or bustling, I can promise you this: Restoring order to this nexus of family activity will enhance your enjoyment of household life.

6
The Living Room

My friend Molly and I loved the couch in my parents' living room. It wasn't just your standard couch. It was a bright royal blue sectional couch with a bulbous round island at the end. It was the not-so-understated anchor of our living room that our friends found quite hilarious. The upholstered cushions were so puffed up they looked like inflated brioche rolls just waiting to be deflated. Molly and I made up endless dance routines in the living room to the *Annie* soundtrack or the latest song we were learning in choir, and then we gleefully pounced on the puffy-looking cushions. Our pouncing was followed by moaning as we remembered how rock hard those cushions really were.

Our living room was also the site of the annual Easter festivities and egg hunt. Our Easter baskets always lined the hearth right where the Bunny had left them. I don't know if I should be embarrassed to tell you this or not, but to this day my parents still put on an annual hunt for me and my husband. I'd like to say it's for them, but I'll be honest. I know all of my mom's hiding spots, and since Trevor is so good at so many things, I enjoy this delicious opportunity to crush him at something at least once a year. Yes, I am normally the Easter Egg Hunt Champion. After my parents finally redecorated the living room and converted it into an actual family room, I worked hard to adjust to the new hiding spots. But I've been able to adapt.

When we hosted distant relatives or other people for whom my brother and I had to be on good behavior, the living room was also the destination of choice. My parents sat in the velour chairs or on the voluptuous couch and visited with our guests. My brother and I sat until our eyes glazed over, and then we offered to get something from the kitchen. However infrequently these visits occurred, the living room was the place strangers congregated as far as I was concerned.

Other than hosting strangers, Easter activities, and the occasional dance routine, our oversized living room usually sat empty. We passed it a hundred times a day but rarely used it. Endless shelves held rows and rows of knickknacks that my mom collected. From glass butterflies to Hummel figurines to odds and ends collected at flea markets, everything was on display for the strangers and Easter Bunny to enjoy.

Neglected Room

If family frequently uses your living room and everything in it, then you may not need to consider a reorganization. If you actually do entertain in this room or use it in some other way that is serving a practical purpose, by all means keep your living room intact. Very often living rooms are deserted spaces. This chapter is for those who find that their living room is dead weight and want to put it to better use.

Perhaps you can relate to the neglected living room phenomenon. Maybe you grew up in a home where the living room was an afterthought. I've found that those of us who grew up with wasted real estate in our living rooms often commit to *really using* our living rooms or even buying homes that don't have living rooms because we are convinced they would be abandoned.

As I've polled my friends about the living rooms they grew up with, most have shared my experience that the space was reserved for holidays and visitors. They have vague memories of antiques stored inside. Some had a piano in the living room, which drew a crowd during their childhood lessons or again at Christmastime for caroling. Otherwise, almost all agreed that their living room was the least used room in their home. My current neighbors are from the South, and they commented that their living rooms almost always had a door you could shut, thereby isolating this room even more from the rest of the home.

Sometimes the names "living room" and "family room" are used interchangeably. My Southern friends even call this room the "den." However, I should clarify that when I am talking about a living room, I mean a formal space, often adjacent to a dining room. In older floor plans this room is often called a parlor or a salon. The intention was to create a gathering space, a sitting room, and a space in which to socialize. It used to be common for friends to gather and discuss politics or the issues of the day. Unfortunately, these days families seem to spend more time watching television than conversing. As a result, the living room often sits empty while the hub of family life gravitates to the family room.

Usual Pitfalls

Knickknack Purgatory

During my childhood, I found that other people stored a lot of collectibles and knickknacks in their living rooms too. My friends' parents seemed to have the same affection for knickknacks my own parents had. Maybe our parents decided to fan their special belongings out in rooms they didn't want us playing in. Perhaps they kept a lot of delicate items on the surfaces so they could tell us: "No roughhousing! Just look at all these things. I don't want you to break anything!"

During my career as an organizer, I have been in hundreds of living rooms, most of which were relatively unused. In these quiet rooms,

I've observed that people love to display their possessions. Perhaps these items are hand-me-downs they don't know where else to store in the household. Perhaps the knickknacks are indeed too breakable to be stored in more frequented rooms.

Of course, to store our collections, we purchase special furniture. We buy lighted curio cabinets, shelving systems, sideboards, and hutches. Pretty soon, our living rooms become museums of things we rarely look at in a room we rarely visit. Apparently we just like to display our possessions in these rooms. Why? I don't know. Maybe we want to show the strangers and the Easter Bunny what good taste we have. Maybe we want to impress people who visit. You've got to wonder why we need all these things that just take up space in our homes.

I should clarify that I'm not against having collections or displaying your favorite things. As a matter of fact, I have a teacup collection I've been adding to since high school. I enjoy grouping patterns together and admiring the colorful gleaming porcelain. I invite my guests to choose cups that catch their fancy for their own special cup of tea. Other than teacups and teapots, I do not collect anything else. Here's what I've discovered in my home and in others' homes: Limited collections and display items are comforting; they can make you feel as if you are surrounded by old friends. On the flip side, if your home is overflowing with collections and knickknacks, it will look cluttered and disorganized very quickly.

Dust Collector

My brother and I were given weekly chores. To be fair, the duties switched off from week to week as we drew them from a bowl. I secretly hoped to draw "set the table" since I liked arranging the dishes and utensils and napkins creatively. Both my brother and I detested any of the chores associated with dusting, especially in the rooms whose surfaces were covered with stuff. The poor sap who drew "dust the living room" had to carefully remove each and every one of those knickknacks from the glass or wooden shelves, remember its placement, dust the shelf with the appropriate glass or wood cleaner, dust the collectible, and reset the army of knickknacks. Even weeding the yard began to look attractive to the kid stuck with dusting the living room.

Inevitably, displays invite layers of dust. The more surfaces you have, the more dust catchers you have put in place! I suppose one benefit to seldom visiting the living room is that you just don't notice the dust. Eventually, however, you will need to dust to prevent embarrassment and allergies. If your living room is serving as little more than a museum and a dust collector, ask yourself if you really want it to stay that way. Dusting a room that you use all the time is bad enough, but dusting a room that no one uses seems like an enormous waste of time.

In my view, organizing your home is about making room in your life (and your space) for that which is important to you *now*, not what *used to be* important to you or what *might* become important to you. Ordering your home gives you the opportunity to reconsider how you've been using your space and to reconfigure your home for optimal use. Many people look at their neglected living rooms in the organizing process and decide to reclaim them for better use.

Staging Area

Molly and I had reasons for using the living room to choreograph dance routines. First, no one else was ever in there! Second, despite the massive blue couch and endless shelves of knickknacks, the room had lots of floor space. This expansive floor space can be inviting in overcrowded and disorganized homes. As a result, the living room can become victimized by the overflow of other rooms.

When the living room is not well used and has no defined purpose, it can become a staging area. Think about it: When you need to assemble a doll house or new foosball table, where do you go? To the place where you can spread out! When you are sorting boxes of files or toys or books or giveaway items, where do you go? To the room with the most floor space!

Our organizers are often asked to help organize living rooms in this staging state, and our recommendation is not always popular. Sure, we could help you put your staged items in short-term storage, but this would simply be tidying. And as we have seen, tidying is not the same as organizing. If you are using your living room as a staging area we would advise you to figure out the purpose of the living room. Do you want to continue using it as a museum? Or do you want to reclaim it for another use? Are you envisioning a home office or game room in this neglected space? Once you know how you will set up and use this room, you will want to protect its new purpose and guard against invaders.

New Purposes

If you have a neglected or ill-used living room, I invite you to consider alternative ways to use the room. Making purposeful use of your space is a crucial step in organizing your home. Especially in smaller homes, this means capitalizing on all available real estate. How else could your living room be used? What purposes do you need your home to serve that you just don't seem to have enough space for now? What will you do with your knickknacks and collections and furniture that are currently in the room?

If you are ready to change and to say goodbye to your living room, these may be easy decisions for you. Making more practical use of your space is a sensible choice. In the pruning process, I recommend finding charities and consignment shops that would be delighted to receive your belongings. Online auction sites and advertising sites like craigslist are also great resources when you are clearing out.

If you are a sentimental packrat, however, even the thought of having to make these decisions may inflict pain. Remember, I'm not encouraging you to dump the things that are meaningful to you. Organizing is not about depriving you of your special things. I would never want to make someone feel as if something special was being taken away from them. My goal is not to force you to let go. On the contrary, I want to help you make room for that which *is* important to you. I believe in surrounding yourself with things of beauty and utility (remember my beloved teacups). Yet sometimes we are surrounded by so much stuff we can't even think, and the clutter begins to close in on us.

If you look at organizing as making room for your very important things, you may be more willing to part with other less important things. By doing so, you will empower yourself to eliminate superfluous stuff and reclaim your home. Neglected living room knickknacks have (perhaps unconsciously) been assigned a place of less importance than other belongings that are used and enjoyed daily. Use the clues of where you have placed things in your home to help you start pruning back your belongings.

Making Up for Limited Space

As you begin pruning your long-forgotten belongings in the living room to make way for a new purpose, think about the space that you lack in the rest of your home. If you have a smaller home and all your bedrooms are committed to children, you may have no work space for Mom and Dad. Could you reclaim your living room as a home office? If your kids' toys are bursting out of their bedrooms, could you turn the living room into a playroom? One caution, though: When you are considering activities that could be relocated to the former living room, be sure to consider its location. If the living room cannot be concealed and is the first room people see when they enter the house, perhaps you do not want computers or toys there.

Dining Hall

If your neglected living room is adjacent to your kitchen and you don't have a dining room, evaluate your kitchen space carefully. Has your family outgrown the tiny breakfast nook? Does the kitchen provide enough seating for larger parties? How often do you have dinner guests anyway? Would it make sense to combine the two rooms to make an enlarged, more serviceable space? If the two rooms could be joined inexpensively, or if you could convert the living room into a separate dining room, would it be worth it?

In the next chapter we will discuss dining rooms. Unfortunately, the dining room is often an infrequently used space also, so swapping one neglected room for another won't help. Yet some people have a formal living room right next to the kitchen, and even though they never step foot in the living room, they would never have thought to create a dining room. In the right home with the right layout, simply replacing the carpet with a spill-safe flooring and moving the table can turn a deserted living room into a lively dining hall. See chapter 7 to read about my own kitchen and dining room combination. By thinking outside your intended floor plan, you can establish rooms that work for you!

Homework Study

As children become teenagers, our organizers frequently create spaces for the older kids to study. Often the access to a computer in a home office or kitchen hub is limited. If three kids want to do their homework on one computer, household harmony is disrupted. Yet we always encourage our clients to keep computers with Internet access *out* of children's bedrooms or rooms with a door. Kids of any age can become victim to the wave of predators that now exist in cyberspace. But with no computers in their private spaces and limited access to the family computer, teens really do face difficulty in completing their homework these days, especially now that so much online research is required.

A smart solution to the homework challenge is to create a homework study in a public area. The idea is to give kids a space where they can store their reference material and school supplies, spread out on a work surface, and use a computer, all the while being supervised (or at least within easy view). Sometimes we set a desk up in a family room or a wide hallway for this purpose. If you are thinking about finding a new purpose for your dusty living room, its very public nature and open access might be an ideal destination for a homework center for your kids.

Special-Interest Room

Each family's unique personality can be reflected in its home. If your family loves music, for example, perhaps you could convert your living room into a music studio. Whenever I see a piano in a home, I ask the family about how often it is played and by whom. Sadly, too often these beautiful instruments are gleaming surfaces that collect dust! If that is your situation, and you want to get back into playing, perhaps you could use the piano to anchor your studio. If this idea sparks excitement for you, run with it! Gather all the musical instruments throughout the house, set up a few music stands with sheet music, and create a room that can encourage the musical genius of your family! Even families who don't play music might enjoy a room dedicated to listening to it, complete with stereo equipment, records, tapes, or CDs.

I don't have a musical bone in my body, and I basically just try to blend when I'm singing at church, so creating a music room wouldn't entice me in the slightest. However, I do like to read. I have since I was a child. I could really get into having a library. If I had a neglected room to convert into another purpose, I can just picture a room lined with shelves and books of all descriptions. Of course, my library would be categorized by type, and my old collectible children's books, like my Nancy Drew series, would hold a place of honor. I can smell their old pages even now. I would have a section for poetry and leadership and business books and Bibles and devotionals, and the list goes on! My library would be made complete with a wood-burning fireplace and a chair with an ottoman.

Do you see where I'm headed? You will begin to *want* to organize your home and reclaim unused space when you begin to be inspired by your own priorities and interests. Many organizing efforts fail because we try to model our homes after something we've seen in a magazine or some advice we thought we should take. We've tried to make things perfect. We've done what works for other people. I promise you this (because I've seen it work hundreds of times): When you create a home that really works for you and your priorities, you will break through to a state of order you can enjoy and sustain.

7

The Dining Room

MOST MODERN HOMES COME WITH a formal dining room in addition to a kitchen nook. Who really uses the dining room? Now, I know we like to use our dining rooms at Thanksgiving and Christmas and Easter, but I've seen a lot of dust and clutter collecting in dining rooms throughout the rest of the year. Dining rooms are like guest bedrooms; we all think we need one, but the truth is most of us just don't use them very much.

Rose has a formal dining room as well as a kitchen table for her family of five. Her dining room has a lovely bay window and accommodates a big table, upholstered chairs, and a huge hutch stocked with china. She loves that room even though she rarely has guests. But the dining room table often attracts projects and clutter that have nowhere else to go in the household. The floor collects bags of items to be returned and holiday decorations that are being staged for setup or teardown. Essentially, her dining room has become a dumping ground. The clutter annoys Rose, but she accepts it as a way of life. She clears it out and entertains once a year—at Easter. (All the other holidays are claimed by other family members.)

As I have been working on organizing projects throughout Rose's home, I've noticed that she has paper everywhere, flung from the kitchen table to the dining room to the basement to the garage. Big jars of pens and pencils are stationed throughout the house. Rose doesn't have a single file cabinet or even a set of trays to process incoming paper. As a result, the paper continues to grow in vertical stacks on every available surface. Her daughters have a homework area upstairs, but Rose has no home office.

I have been trying for months to convince Rose to convert her dining room, which gets used once a year, into a home office, which would be used daily. We cannot overcome Rose's paper problem without a dedicated space to operate her household and deal with documents. Rose is handicapped without a household business center. She cannot get ahead of the dumping, stacking, piling, and stashing in her home. I can just envision an office outfitted with work space and cabinets and drawers, all customized to her personal tastes. I can imagine her daughters coming in the room and enjoying the space with her while she works.

So far, Rose has defended that dumping ground of a dining room and has resisted my reasoning. She doesn't even really like the dining room furniture, but she feels obligated to retain a space where she can entertain if she feels like it. Even though she is a very busy professional woman, she has visions of entertaining more than she currently does. Rose struggles to let go of the *idea* of having a dining room.

If Rose had a home office, she wouldn't miss the dining room at all. When Easter rolled around, she could set up tables in the living room and present her big family meal with as much joy and style as she does now. I'm going to keep working on Rose. I believe that when you stop serving the constraints of your home and instead set it up to serve you, you can derive a whole new level of enjoyment from your living space.

To Keep or Not to Keep?

One way to help you decide if you actually need your dining room is to ask yourself how frequently you use it. If the answer is three times a year or less, are you sure you need to reserve a room for the sole purpose of formal entertaining? Could you entertain elsewhere on the rare occasion that you have multiple guests? Most importantly, if you are strapped for space in the rest of your house, are you willing to preserve your dining room but forsake having a room you would use more often?

Other considerations might help you decide whether to ditch the dining room. If you have two spaces for eating, you could consolidate those spaces and free up the dining room. For example, if you have a kitchen table or counter that comfortably seats your family, plus an occasional friend or two, then you may not even need a dining room. Many homes have two tables of generous size, but the one in the dining room rarely gets used. If that is your situation, you might consider whether you should keep your dining room intact or convert it to another more useful purpose. Organizing your home is about purposely creating space that makes sense for the way you and your family really live. Unfortunately, however, many of us unconsciously adapt to the space we've been given instead of making it work for us.

Of course, if you commonly entertain large groups, you may want to retain the dining room for that purpose. If you are the only member of your extended family who has a dining room, you will likely attract all the relatives at every holiday. Folks who host small groups from church or the local Boy Scout troop often enjoy having a dining room for mealtime and for spreading out materials to work together. People who love to throw parties actively use their dining rooms. If entertaining is your thing, you will probably keep your dining room so your household can serve your actual lifestyle.

You may also want to keep your dining room intact if you only have one table, you have no room for it in or near the kitchen, and it permanently resides in the dining room. In that instance, the dining room is really serving as your daily eating area, and eliminating it wouldn't make sense. Every home needs at least one space where the family can come together around the dinner table. The conversation and fellowship you enjoy when you eat together are among your most precious treasures.

Common Traps

If you are going to keep your dining room because you've determined that you need it or can't bear to part with it, please at least reserve it for its intended purpose: eating and entertaining. To help you in this endeavor, I want to share with you some of the common traps I've seen that cause disorder in this space.

Paper Parking Lot

The most inviting trap is to use your dining room table surface as a dumping ground for the mail, an archive for kids' school papers, and a substitute for a filing system. After all, we figure that this huge surface should get used for something! Many dining rooms feature a dining room table that's completely buried. The wood grain hasn't been seen in years because the table surface serves as a mailbox! If you use your table as a landing spot for paper of all descriptions, this habit is indicative that you need a home office elsewhere. If you also have a home office, something isn't working! You may be missing the step of successfully transferring incoming paper to the right location within the home office, or perhaps your home office is missing some key systems, like paper processing or filing.

Hand-Me-Down Haven

What do you do with grandma's ugly china that you inherited? Are you keeping 25 huge silver serving pieces that are not your style and that you would never use? If you can't bear the thought of washing and rewashing stemware, why are you keeping two sets of 12? So often, our dining rooms become museums of generations gone by. It's time to evaluate all your hand-me-downs and even items you received as gifts that are no longer "you" and make some tough decisions.

There are alternatives to storing stuff that plagues you with guilt and takes up valuable space. If you have serving dishes or memorabilia that you don't want, consider offering them to a more sentimental family member or to someone who appreciates their style more than you. After you've checked with all concerned family and no one wants the items, you can let yourself off the guilt hook. Go online and look at all the auction sites like eBay and craigslist and find out what price you can fetch for your unwanted items. Take them to consignment. Donate them. Sell them at a garage sale. Organizing is about making room in your life for that which is important *now*, not what was important in the past or what might *be* important someday. Go on and free yourself. Your great aunt would rather you have room for the things that are precious to you than the things that used to be important to her.

If you're going to really use your dining room, avoid the paper parking lot and hand-me-down haven. When you designate your dining room for eating and entertaining, you'll want to keep the items that serve those purposes nearby. Items like table linens, candles, stemware, serving pieces, and silver often live in dining room hutches and sideboards. Padded fabric dish containers offer safe storage for your china. Foam squares also make great separators for service ware. Of course, you may be limited in what you can store by the furniture you have, so just begin with the most important items that serve the primary purposes, and add other items that make sense as your space increases.

Alternative Uses

What if you've decided that you don't want to keep your dining room or—for the less bold—that you might be open to eliminating it? Ditching your dining room might seem scary, so I want to share with you some successful and encouraging conversions I've participated in. And if you're worried about what you will do with a crowd without a dining room, don't forget the options of setting up extra tables, buffet-style dining, TV trays, and outdoor dining. Of course, if you know you must keep your dining room, then read the next section just for fun.

Floor-Plan Swap

I have a home with a pretty typical floor plan. It includes a living room–dining room combination. It's one long room with no dividing walls. A chandelier hangs over the dining room half. When I first moved in, that is exactly how I used it. I placed a couch at an angle to divide the long room into two smaller rooms. My dining room table sat over the lovely white carpet (one of many first-time homeowner mistakes) at the far end of the room. I only used the table for big meals once or twice a year.

Adjacent to my kitchen is a tiny room that has a fireplace in it. The floor plan called it the family room. Dutifully, when I moved in, I crammed a couch and loveseat into the small space. I didn't have room for a coffee table, and the crowding of furniture created a narrow passageway between my kitchen counter and couch. Whenever I had guests over, which I love to do, some would gravitate to the family room but it only offered about five seats at best. Once that was full, all the other guests were stuck out in the living room. I didn't like the way this layout affected the togetherness of my guests.

Eventually, I decided to rip up all the carpet and lay hardwood floors throughout the downstairs to create an easy flow. I moved the dining room table onto the hardwood in front of the fireplace, creating a lovely sprawling kitchen. I situated my matching sideboard inside the new "dining room." The combination of wood floor and less furniture opened up the room and defined the space for one primary purpose: preparing and eating meals. We love adding leaves to our table and seating a dozen people in front of a roaring fire at the holidays. Trevor and I sometimes sit at the table and play games, and we often have our neighbors over for festive drinks and appetizers.

If you are as unsatisfied with your dining room as I was, begin thinking about how you might be able to reconfigure your floor plan to better serve you. Think about traffic flow and how your guests experience your space. I spoke with several girlfriends about my ideas before I did the swap, and you may want to solicit the input of people who know your home well to affirm your reimagined space.

Practical Home Office

My friends Mike and Annie also had a dining room that wasn't being used properly. In fact, they didn't even have a dining table in the room. Kids' toys cluttered the floor, and two makeshift tables served as desks. An old rickety nightstand held a printer, and a wooden bench stored a collection of photos and frames. Mike and Annie have limited real estate in their home, so they needed to make better use of the space that the builder had intended for a dining room.

Mike and Annie had such an interesting challenge that I featured their project on the Home and Garden Television (HGTV) show *Mission: Organization.* We decided to convert their dining space into a full-fledged home office. After measuring the space, we created various stations for the purposes the room was to serve. Annie needed the most work space for her graphic design business, and we wanted a workstation for Mike and his laptop. Additionally, the photos, oversized paper, and drawing supplies had nowhere else to live, so we also needed a creative station inside the home office.

In the end, we installed built-in workspaces around the periphery of the room, each station customized around Mike and Annie's actual use. We also installed French doors in the open archway for privacy and to delineate this room as an adult space. Their former dining room took on new life. The floor is no longer strewn with their kids' toys. They now conduct their personal and professional business out of this room, and they love its look and function.

A home office is one of the most essential and most often used spaces in the home. If you lack the space for an effective home office elsewhere in your home, look to your dining room to see if you can reclaim the real estate for this purpose.

Nearby Playroom

Darla is a client whose children are two, four, and five. Little ones unconsciously tend to play near Mom and Dad. Often, that means they drag their dolls and trucks into the kitchen to be near you. I call this a gravitational pull toward "centers of community," and I discuss these dynamics in chapter 13 of *Reclaim Your Life.*

Darla's kitchen is right next to her dining room. She had two tables, one in each room. She and the family used the smaller table in the kitchen and intended to use the formal set in the dining room for entertaining, yet they hardly ever used the dining room. As Darla's kids were continually gravitating toward the kitchen and the outlying areas were becoming full of toys, she began to reconsider the use of these two important rooms.

First, Darla and her husband remodeled their kitchen. They installed a long island with a huge counter for family breakfasts. Six or eight stools fit comfortably along the counter, so they had room for friends as well. Next, they upgraded their round kitchen table to a rectangular shape that had three leaves. Soon they had room to seat 12 people at their expandable kitchen table and up to 8 more at barstool seats. They could now comfortably seat 20 in their kitchen for holiday meals, so Darla was anxious to eliminate the dining room, which was simply collecting dust.

She had just sold her dining room set when I came into the picture. We had a nice rectangular room with big windows to work with. I stepped over many toys on the way to the empty room and soon affirmed that converting the dining room into a playroom was an excellent idea. She painted the walls a cheery yellow, and we began establishing little neighborhoods of fun for her kids. Soon, all the trucks and cars and robots and dolls and arts and crafts and dress-up clothes had a new home, and everyone settled right into the new arrangement. Darla has told me several times since our project how much she enjoys having her kids nearby but in their own space.

Light and Bright Studio

Perhaps the most unique conversion I've seen is the metamorphosis of an unused dining room into a full-fledged art studio. Born with an eye for decorating and a love of making things, Jenny is constantly looking for ways to be creative. Jenny is already pretty organized, but she wanted a little help executing her ideas for her home. She had already begun a dining room conversion when our organizer arrived on the scene.

Jenny told us that her inspiration to make the dining room into her art studio was the fantastic lighting. Indeed, sunshine floods in from the big picture windows at the end of the room. It is a cheerful, well-lit room that wasn't meeting its potential as a dining room, and Jenny needed easily accessible space for her creative outlet.

First, Jenny pulled up the carpet and installed vinyl floors. She painted the walls a lovely periwinkle. She was on a roll, and all our organizer needed to do was help her figure out how to fit all of her many forms of art into the small room! We worked with Jenny to establish categories: painting, glazing, card making, and pottery. We determined the best storage for each kind of supply and determined the placement of her tools and equipment. We lined the walls with easy-access storage while retaining the airy feel of the room.

Jenny's dining room conversion may help you think outside the box. Her project was pretty bold in my opinion. Her former dining room, now an art studio, connects to her living room, so you can see through the living room into this funky, functional space. A lot of people wouldn't take that risk. They would think about the practical concerns of reselling their home and the flow of the two rooms together. They would find a million reasons to talk themselves out of putting an art studio into a dining room. But not Jenny. I am so proud of her boldness. Every time I see her I ask what she's been working on in her studio lately. Her eyes light up as she shows me her most recent creations.

You probably have some great ideas like Jenny's. Don't be afraid to talk about them with your friends or with your organizer and work toward making them a reality!

Room for Hospitality

By now you've probably decided whether you are going to keep or ditch your dining room. If you've determined to keep the space intact, sidestep the traps I've shared so that you can get the most enjoyment from your dining room. If you are ready to eliminate the dining room, I hope you've been inspired and emboldened by some successful conversions.

When I think of dining rooms, I think of sparkling stemware and the chime of holiday toasts among a dozen or more guests. I think of the steaming turkey and gleaming china. Maybe you think of those things too. The romantic idea of a dining room can make us think that we have to have all the perfect trappings to be hospitable. But let's get real. Sometimes Christmas dinner is held at a restaurant. Sometimes birthday parties are in the backyard with scores of children. Sometimes all you can muster at Thanksgiving is a store-bought meal. None of those meals have to be any less special than if they were served at a mahogany table with a lace cloth and china service. Entertaining guests shouldn't be as much about the presentation as it should be about the people.

You can be hospitable on paper plates served on that mahogany table. Hospitality can be choosing a favorite dish for a friend and serving it simply. Hospitality is the gift of yourself that you give to others. Yes, it might involve serving food in your dining room, but it also might be about the warmth with which you greet people, even if your home is a mess. Hospitality is a spirit you can extend to all who you encounter, a spirit that says, "Welcome, you are loved." It's a spirit that invites belonging, togetherness, and friendship. Once you get that dining room (or office, playroom, or studio) organized the way you like it, don't forget to make room for hospitality.

The Playroom

Recently I worked with a family that insisted that the children put their toys away in their rooms each night. Their father told me, "They can play with a few things at a time, but they have to put them away when they're done. We want to use the family room for the family at night and not be tripping over their stuff." He seemed surprised by my prolific praise, but I was truly impressed. This family was drawing a line between family-use and kid-use space and setting expectations for their children. What's more impressive, their children were obeying! As you might suspect, this family is an anomaly among my clients!

If that scenario seems too good to be true, you're not alone! Most of our clients find that their children's belongings travel throughout the house. Parents everywhere are thwarted by nomadic kid stuff and feel overwhelmed by the sheer number of rooms that are buried under layers of toys. Kids' bedrooms are definitely hot spots, and I address them in part 3. Many homes these days also have a recreation room, bonus room, family room, or playroom where kids can store and play with their toys. In this chapter I am referring to the primary location of your kid's playthings as the playroom, even if you have converted your dining room or family room to this purpose. If you have several rooms that have been taken over by kid gear, perhaps by the end of this chapter you will be inspired to consolidate rooms and prune the overage.

Depending on where the playroom is located within the home, you might consider it a public or a private space. If it is in an easily accessible space that is highly trafficked, it might be by nature a more public room. Also, if your kids often invite their friends over to play, the room takes on a more public nature. On the other hand, if the playroom is situated in a small bedroom upstairs, it might seem more private to you. I am considering the playroom as a public space because kids and their toys often attract other kids!

When I was little, my mom wanted our friends to come to our house rather than the other way around so she could keep her eye on us! This way, she always knew our friends and could supervise. The result was that my brother and I often had friends over whether we were playing in the yard, in the attic, or in our bedrooms. One reason to establish a safe, pared-down playroom is that an appealing space can keep the attention of your own children and attract other children as well.

Safety

The first concern of a playroom is not how it is decorated or arranged or equipped. Your children's safety is the first issue at hand. From securing furniture to installing locks and latches to observing safety measures, it's up to you to hazard-proof the play center of your home.

If you have little climbing monkeys, for example, you will want to choose immoveable, heavy furniture or bolt it to the floor or wall so it cannot be toppled. Toy chests and cabinets with swinging doors should be child-proofed with latches that hold doors open so that little heads are not inadvertently banged. Of course, you'll want to prevent toxic, sharp, or otherwise dangerous items from entering the playroom at all. Every playroom should be set up in an age-appropriate way so that your children only have access to the things you want them to use.

Toys

One of the primary complaints our organizers hear from parents is the frustration of toys taking over a household. Kids have more toys today than ever before. Sure, I had some Strawberry Shortcake dolls and Barbies, but I didn't have so many belongings that I couldn't keep track of them. Many factors contribute to the common problem of traveling toys, but two reasons stand out the most: having an overabundance of toys and not limiting where kids play with and store them.

Toy Gluttony

If you are not convinced that your children have too many toys, I recommend you go into their bedrooms and playroom when they are out. Begin counting their stuffed animals and dolls. Then count their arts and crafts supplies: coloring books, crayons, paints, project kits, sewing kits, construction paper, glues, and glitters. If you are still not convinced, count their games, puzzles, and cards next. Add up their robots, plastic animals, action figures, and collectibles. Don't forget the freebie toys they've collected at birthday parties and in fast-food meals. Also remember the structures: like dollhouses, carports, airports, and train stations. Outdoor toys cannot be overlooked either, including plastic swimming pools, child-sized lawn chairs, wagons, buckets, bikes, shovels, rakes, trikes, Slip 'n Slides, and the like. If you catch my drift, most of our accumulation on behalf of our children is a bit unconscious. Just becoming aware of the quantity you have can be a catalyst to prune back and prevent future excesses.

We all want our children to have the best in life. We want them to have a memorable childhood, and we often think that has to do with the amount of stuff we give them. But remember when we were kids? When I was growing up, I loved playing with my baking set on the floor in the kitchen. My brother and I made forts with the pillows of the couch. We jumped from couch to couch playing Hot Lava Monster. I ran around in our yard and used my imagination, playing house among the tree trunks and imagining I was one of the characters from my favorite books like Heidi or Pippi Longstocking. Some of my fondest memories are in our old camper. My parents took us to every KOA on the West Coast, I think. We thought we were cool for riding in the bed above the cab while the camper was moving. I read thousands of pages as we put miles on that camper. As we got older, we brought friends with us, roasted marshmallows, and played poker with toothpicks. My point is this: Yes, we had some toys and electronics growing up, but not so many that we couldn't enjoy the outdoors and the simple pleasures of life. Which would you rather have for your children?

I don't claim to be a psychologist or parenting expert, but from what I've seen in people's homes, kids who have way too much stuff seem to get overstimulated and don't appreciate their belongings as much as children who have fewer toys and are expected to care for them. If you or your family members have been supplying an overload of toys for your children, you can do several things to backtrack. Of course, any approach you take should be appropriate to your children's age and temperament.

First, you can do a major pruning. For more on the Pruning Principle, see chapter 10 of *Reclaim Your Life*. You can trim back the superfluous games, toys, and knickknacks that are crowding their bedrooms and playrooms. You may want to involve them; I've seen this become a very positive activity, especially if you get them excited about donating the overage to kids who don't have any toys. This approach enhances your children's awareness of all their blessings and the fact that other children have much less than they do.

After pruning back the deadwood, you can also take up to half their toys and put them in bins and hide them away, rotating them seasonally. When you decide to reintroduce the toys, you can box up the current toys and whisk them away, preferably while your kids are out, and replace them with the "forgotten" toys. This provides a fresh experience of "new" toys for them. (Of course, leave their favorite stuffed animals or precious treasures year-round so as not to cause trauma!)

Lastly, you can politely ask family members for different kinds of gifts in the future, like adding to a special collection of books. Alternatively, Grandma and Grandpa can make a gift to their college savings. One of my favorite ideas is to give experiences as gifts instead of stuff. Any loved one can give your child a "date day," like a promise of a special outing with them. Gift certificates for the ice cream or movie store are also increasingly popular as your child ages.

Boundary-Challenged

No one likes to step on toys in the hallway or slip on doll clothes in the kitchen. Yet toys tend to show up all over the home. Most often, this sneaky spread is the result of not limiting kid space and not honoring boundaries.

The main reason toys creep is that children play with them in multiple locations. Our organizers help parents determine where children should store and play with their toys. Many times, children use their playthings in their bedrooms, the family room, the living room, the playroom, the hallway, and all over the house. If we can choose one primary location where children should play with and store their toys (like a playroom or bonus room), we will begin to make progress.

Of course, special toys, like models that a child has carefully assembled or favorite teddy bears, should likely live in each child's bedroom so they are safe. Community-use objects like blocks and games and big plastic toys can live in the playroom. You may have to make this decision solely on the space you have available. If you don't have the luxury of a kid-friendly room like a playroom or bonus space, then all toys might need to be stored in the children's individual rooms.

Limiting where your children store and play with toys is not meant to be a rigid rule; it's meant to help you streamline your kids' play and storage. You may want your kids to have a playroom but also to keep a toy chest in the family room so they can play near you while you're in the kitchen. The point is to be more thoughtful about not letting *every* room become a playroom. When kids don't have one primary storage place for their toys and are allowed to keep them out in multiple rooms, they don't naturally conclude that they should put toys away because they simply don't know where they go!

Another strategy for controlling the spread of toys is limiting the number of toys that can come out to play at once and deciding how often you expect your children to return all toys to their proper destination. One of my good friends has two toddlers, and she has the kids put their toys away before their nap and before bedtime. This boundary helps her keep the tidal wave of toys at bay.

The children and the household suffer if parents pick up the toys for the children. Whether to avoid a fight or to save time, many parents just cave and act as the cleanup crew for their children. Kids are good at training adults, and if they see you picking up their belongings, they will think that is the norm and relieve themselves of that responsibility. These kids are likely to grow up into adults who expect their spouse or boss to pick up after them too!

I once heard that *responsibility* simply means our response to our ability. If you teach kids to pick up after themselves or use one thing at a time they are young, even when their abilities are limited, you will be sowing positive seeds that you will reap later when they are older and their abilities increase. Think about it: Many of the things we don't like doing as adults are the things that require constant maintenance like dishes and laundry. If we don't pick up after ourselves as adults, our household dissolves into chaos. If we observe boundaries around our chores, however, our household works better, and we get to keep our sanity! Help your children set and honor boundaries now so that in the future they will be well-equipped to run their households and their lives.

Neighborhoods

The playroom is like a little city filled with various neighborhoods. Many big cities are distinguished by neighborhoods featuring different activities, such as the shopping district and the fashion district. Try thinking of the playroom jungle as a city that you can divide into different neighborhoods.

Your specific playroom neighborhoods will depend on the interests and ages of your children. Arts and crafts are popular for children of almost any age (except in later high school, when makeup and cars generally take precedence). If your kids like to do crafts, consider setting up a creative district with a table and supplies nearby. The supplies will change as your kids become more responsible and safe. Things like scissors and glue can be entrusted to older children but would be a disaster in the hands of young ones.

A reading district might be compelling to your children if they like to read inside their playroom and if that's where most of their books are stored. In some cases, however, kids' books are stored with all the other books in the household, so this neighborhood might not make sense in your home.

Little girls might be enamored with their very own fashion district, complete with a trunk of fancy dress-up clothes and costumes. From funky shoes to feather boas to engineer hats to shell necklaces, dress-up areas often attract even little boys with their potential for make-believe and fun.

Little boys may need a transportation district, where all the trains, cars, trucks, tractors, and planes can come into the station. From depot to carport, boys love things that move and haul stuff! I've often used rugs that have a landscape of streets to anchor the transportation neighborhood in playrooms I've organized.

Your neighborhoods can be as creative as you are. Remember when the Super Friends like Superman, Batman, Green Lantern, Wonder Woman, Aquaman, the Flash, and the Wonder Twins congregated at the Hall of Justice? How about creating a hero district for all your kids' action figures, robots, and related toys? Wouldn't that be a fun place for them to imagine all kinds of drama unfolding?

Of course, don't forget to use the strategies we discussed in part 1 to help you sort and categorize the contents of your playroom if you are starting over from scratch. Most importantly, keep the ages and preferences of your kids in mind, and involve them every step of the way. Their involvement will seal their sense of ownership, which you can capitalize on as you recruit them to honor and maintain their space.

Evaluating Habits (Yours)

When we think about organizing a playroom, we may be tempted to analyze our children's habits. Do they step on toys and break them? Do they climb all over the furniture? Do they draw on the walls and otherwise behave wildly? You certainly should note what is happening in your kids' space and how they are behaving and make modifications accordingly. Yet here's the uncomfortable news: Your kids' space probably has more to do with your habits than theirs.

Your habits may be contributing to a messy playroom more than you realize. I know, this is hard, but as I mentioned earlier in this chapter, if you are buying (or not preventing) a flood of incoming playthings, this habit is likely contributing to the overload both you and your children feel. Likewise, if you have a hard time being con-sistent about boundaries and find yourself giving in all the time and becoming your kids' personal butler, your children will sense that you are pliable (a nice way of saying they can manipulate you) and will begin to take advantage. That's what kids do; they push the envelope so they can feel out their boundaries.

At Christmas our family opened our gifts together. Whenever we opened a gift and the givers were present, we were expected to get off the couch, cross the room, hug them, and thank them for the gift. What's more, we had to follow up with them by writing a nice thank-you card within a month of Christmas. To this day, I am grateful that my parents cultivated in me and my brother an attitude of thankfulness. We were taught from a young age to acknowledge the giver and appreciate the things we were given. In addition, my mom got out bags at the holidays, and we loaded them with old toys and took them to the local Toy and Joy drive for needy children. In giving away our excess, we were made aware that other kids didn't have the nice things we did. It's not too late to begin cultivating in your children an attitude of thankfulness, and doing so will help them to place a greater value on their belongings.

The playroom is the one space in the home that is dedicated to your children. Instead of looking at it as a nuisance that drains your energy, I invite you to view the playroom as a training ground. You can teach new protocols, habits, and attitudes here. This is where your children can learn life skills like organizing, cleaning, storing, and maintaining. If you view the playroom as preparation for your children's future, you may well become more excited about helping them organize and maintain it. Your consistent efforts will pay off in the long run. Our diligence will take root in the soil of our children's lives: "Train a child in the way he should go, and when he is old he will not turn from it" (Proverbs 22:6). It's open training season! Go and let loose your newfound perspective on that unruly playroom!

Part Three

Private Spaces

XXX

Chapter 9: The Bedroom

Chapter 10: The Bathroom

Chapter 11: The Laundry or Utility Room

Chapter 12: The Home Office

Chapter 13: The Hobby Room

XXX

You've just been told that guests will arrive any minute to your messy home. You are appalled, and you don't want them to see inside your world. As you rush around the home, which doors do you shut first? Chances are you can only shut the door on rooms that are reserved for private use, like the bedrooms, bathrooms, laundry room, hobby room, or home office. These spaces are generally used (and abused) by family members who don't always pick up after themselves.

Private spaces are where we conduct the personal business in our lives. Our habits and true selves are laid bare in these spaces. We use our personal rooms to refuel and refresh. Our personal interests and our work are often commingled as we struggle to keep up with our household duties. If you are tired of experiencing frustration and embarrassment over these private spaces, now is the time to restore order!

9
The Bedroom

When I was little, I annoyed my parents by staying up late reading with my flashlight. In the middle of another riveting Nancy Drew book, I couldn't be bothered by "This is the last time I'm telling you. Turn out the lights, Vicki!" I loved my room because it was a little dark cavern at the far end of our basement. Its walls were covered in wood paneling, and I had a cool walk-in closet that I could transform into a ship, fort, dollhouse, secret passageway, or whatever else I dreamed up. I holed away like a mole, reading, organizing, and playing to my heart's content.

My friends came over to help me decorate my room and reorganize my displays. Every so often, we rearranged the furniture in my search for optimal room arrangement. My older brother, Rob, used to love hiding at the bottom of the stairs, so occasionally when I came down the steps unaware, he jumped out from behind the wall with a shout—*Aaagh!*—evoking a terrified scream from me. After one of my room reorganizations, I was chasing my brother down the hall for having scared me, and as he reached my darkened room, he leapt onto the bed for safety—or where the bed used to be. *Crash!* He landed on my rocking chair and decorative end table that had just been placed where the bed used to be! As he rolled around in pain on the floor, I figured he had received his due punishment, and we both collapsed in laughter.

Our bedrooms contain much more than our sleeping quarters. Bedrooms should be places where we refuel and recharge. They should reflect our personalities. Since our tastes change with time, the arrangement and decor and even the furniture of our bedrooms should naturally change as we do.

Master Bedrooms

One of the homes I visited early in my career as a professional organizer had the foulest smell coming from the master bedroom. I wondered if something had actually died in there! One day, I was at the client's home in the evening, working with one of her teens. I saw the mom carrying a dinner tray into the bedroom, where her husband was already tucked into bed, watching television. I asked the teen if her parents frequently ate in their bedroom, and she answered, "Every night." I couldn't believe that someone actually used their master bedroom as their dining room, and I haven't seen such a thing since. I'm sure the mother and father weren't even aware that their habits were resulting in a repulsive odor throughout the home. (Just when you thought you were the worst-case scenario, doesn't that make you feel better?)

The master bedroom should be peaceful and restful, a getaway from life's demands. If at all possible, begin organizing your bedroom by committing to reserve it for its intended purposes. In other words, the master bedroom should not be a dining room, a staging area for unfinished projects, or a mini-storage unit for items you had no room for elsewhere. Let's face it; going to bed surrounded by junk and waking up looking at a big mess is really unpleasant. It can't be good for your mental health!

Some people don't agree with me, but I truly believe that a master bedroom is for the adults in the household. Kids generally have their own or shared bedrooms as well as a playroom or bonus room, and sometimes their belongings creep into the family room, living room, and hallways as well. They just don't need to take over your space too. I've known parents who allow their grade-school children to sleep with them and others who allow their children of all ages to utilize the master bedroom as an alternative playroom.

As I mention in *Reclaim Your Life,* defining the purpose of your space includes creating centers of activity. If kid activities are happening everywhere, children genuinely have no idea where or how to put away their own belongings. If you limit them to a few spaces, you are helping them to set boundaries and take responsibility for themselves. You are also setting a healthy boundary for yourself by reclaiming adult space!

Hot Spots

Like all rooms in the home, master bedrooms tend to have a few hot spots of disorganization. In our adult bedrooms, we tend to unload items we don't know how to deal with, and we accumulate other items that could live elsewhere in the home. To order your bedroom, start by addressing your common dumping areas.

Surfaces are the most common hot spots that receive downloaded items. Tops of dressers and nightstands and any available counter can become obscured by our pocket-emptying habits. As part of our daily download, we drop our wallet, keys, change, sunglasses, and miscellaneous items onto surfaces. Our hats, belts, scarves, and jewelry also land on the runway of our dressers. Even paperwork, to-do lists, grocery lists, and receipts end up on bedroom surfaces. If receipts are found among your piles, you will want to establish a receipt-capture system in your kitchen hub or home office.

When I go through Trevor's surface piles, I often find grocery lists, material lists, and business cards of other contractors with whom he is working. When I show them to him, nine times out of ten he says they can be pitched. (I think I'll put a garbage can by the dresser so he can do it himself!) He is an electrician, so I find wire nuts, wrenches, screwdrivers, electrical tape in all colors, nuts and bolts, Sharpie markers, flat construction pencils, and pens galore. Originally, I had put a small chest on his dresser to capture all of these items along with his wallet, but it had a lid, so he couldn't see into it, and of course, that meant he had to open it before he could dump into it. Apparently this proved too great a challenge, and his pocket download exploded onto the nearby surface.

Always in search of a solution to help reclaim our dresser surfaces, my victory came when I put one of my own products—an attractive metal drawer organizer—on top of his dresser. There is now a spot for hardware, tools, and writing implements. As he deposits, he can now capture like items together and return them to his workbench or work van when the tray gets full. (I'll keep you posted on how long this works.)

Other folks have a chair or valet piled high with clothes and belts and bags. Having a piece of furniture to hold your castoffs is so handy, and you feel better about using it than the floor. The problem is that many of us don't discipline ourselves to clear off the chair daily, so the pile of deposited items simply grows. If you aren't putting things away, your closet and habits may need retooling.

The final frontier of abused bedroom space is the floor. Many use it as an alternative closet. From clothes to shoes, the floor seems to store them all. Some people sort and fold laundry on the floor, they toss their dirty laundry on the floor, and they leave piles of clean laundry on the floor. If you've had a near-death experience as you've tripped on a pair of shoes left askew on the floor, you might be ready to evaluate the habits that are taking place in your master bedroom. In chapter 3 of *Reclaim Your Life*, I explain the five ways by which we become disorganized. One of them is called *habitual disorganization,* whereby we find ourselves surrounded by messes because of a collection of bad habits. If habits need to change in your bedroom, check out that chapter to learn more.

Another hot spot I see in some master bedrooms is a collection of electronics. Some people like to have a television in their room. Many folks, however, get less sleep, stay up too late, and enjoy their spouses less if a blue light and flickering screen keep them company at night. Some of my clients with televisions and video players also store videos in their room. If you store your video players and videos in your bedroom, your kids may want to pile onto your bed (because it's new and different) and watch *their* videos on your television. Pretty soon, their videos stack up in your bedroom. Stereos and cords can add more equipment to our bedrooms as well. Those of us who use hand-held electronic devices and cell phones tend to charge them in our bedrooms, producing a dim green glow.

These hot spots may be bothersome or no big deal to you. The point is this: Think through what you desire to have living in your special private room, and don't allow other things to invade your intended purposes.

Storage Issues

Whenever I organize a master bedroom, clothes crammed in dressers are almost always an issue. Often, dressers store similar items to those that reside in the closet. For that reason, I don't deal with dresser contents independently; I always combine dresser organization with the closet organization.

In addition to dressers, available storage in your bedroom might include a trunk or cedar chest, under-bed real estate, and nightstand drawers and shelves. Some people have bookshelves and other furniture in their master bedrooms, but that's not as common.

Trunks and chests provide excellent storage for pillows, blankets, bed linens, and memorabilia. They also offer a bench to sit on while you remove your shoes. The same handy seating, however, can become a tempting flat surface to dump things on. If you have other items stowed in your trunk, ask yourself whether they really need to live in the bedroom. If not, consider whether the contents should go elsewhere so you can fill it with something you use in the bedroom or whether the whole trunk could move to another room. There aren't any rules about what you should store inside a trunk or chest. The point is to ensure that the contents serve the room in which it is located. (I have an old wooden chest that was once used as a toy box for my brother. I use it in my entry hallway, and we store shoes inside it. Think of ways you can reuse a piece of furniture that is simply taking up space.)

To maximize under-bed real estate, think about what purposes you need the bedroom to serve other than its obvious purposes. We store two foam sleeping pads under our bed since we don't have a guest bed. These pads can be covered with sheets and made into nice little camp beds for our infrequent guests. They take up all the space under the bed placed side by side, so there is no additional room for shoes or clothes to accidentally become kicked underneath and lost. If you have limited storage for bed linens in your hall closet, the inches under your bed can afford space for a few shallow bins to store extra sheets, pillowcases, and blankets. Our organizers often help our clients store out-of-season clothes in these under-bed bins as well.

The nightstand isn't just for holding a lamp and alarm clock; it can serve a variety of other purposes depending on size and storage capacity. Nightstand storage often includes books and extra bed linens. I've also seen collections of all kinds stashed in nightstands. Before yours becomes a dumping ground, think about its necessary uses.

If you like to read at night, storing a few books inside the nightstand makes sense. Just beware that your bedside storage doesn't get out of control. In many of my clients' bedrooms I find a growing library of titles creeping like ivy onto the floor and uphill in stacks. If this is a problem in your bedroom, you may want to designate a location for your library in another room, such as the home office or family room. If you don't have space in those rooms, set up narrow bookshelves in a wide hallway and create a library for family reference. Each shelf can be designated for a specific genre of book: fiction, biographies, travel, entertainment, children's, reference, education, and so on.

Organizing your master bedroom is an investment that will pay you back every night as you turn in and every morning as you awake to peace and order. The up-front investment of time to organize this important room, however, must also be backed by a commitment to process the deposited piles and keep things moving on to their proper destination. Don't allow surface and storage abuse to desecrate your sacred space!

Children's Bedrooms

Discover Interests

Some of our favorite clients are children! Just like an adult, a child has his or her own passions and interests. I enjoy drawing out of children their priorities and interests and helping them to take ownership of their bedrooms. Some kids love animals and nature; others fancy Disney characters; and some collect dolphins, unicorns, robots, or butterflies. Children often have more imagination than adults, and you can tap into their make-believe worlds with a little effort. From board games to sports memorabilia to their own trophies, kids are no different from the rest of us—they want to be surrounded by the things that reflect their tastes and interests.

If you can help your children determine their interests, you will help them narrow down the variety of items they feel they need to keep. Once I've helped a little girl, for example, define her love of horses and princesses, she is so excited about those things that she is more willing to let go of her toys that don't fall into those categories. The same is true for you and me. Once I chose my color theme and the look for my new office, I could eliminate items that didn't fit, and I became more careful about collecting new things that did match my tastes.

Your interests change with time, and your child's interests will too. Pretty soon, she may abandon horses for soccer and her princesses for posters. Use your children's growing maturity to encourage them to let go of neglected toys and interests, but don't force them. When your children are too tiny to have a say, you will have to take charge and make decisions for them so that by the time their interests emerge they won't have to part with all their baby and toddler items as well as the last decade of interests!

Establish Activity Centers

There is a reason a child's classroom works so well. It features centers where certain activities take place, like reading, manipulatives, math, and crafts. You can use this principle when you are helping set up your child's bedroom. This is the same concept as establishing "neighborhoods" as we discussed in the previous chapter.

To help your child organize his or her room, you'll first need to decide whether some or all of the toys will need to live in the bedroom. If you are stuck keeping all toys in your child's bedroom, you will probably need some additional storage and drawers dedicated to this purpose. Under-bed storage, bookshelves, hutches over desks, and even the closet shelving system can provide excellent toy storage.

If you don't mind your children doing certain crafts in their rooms, you can give them an area for that activity. Often, however, many craft projects can be messy. Supervising crafts at the kitchen table or allowing crafts to take place over a vinyl floor might be best, especially if your children are young.

I had a bright pink and white desk with a hutch when I was growing up. The shelves held my Nancy Drew books and my other collections. The deep drawers contained a wide variety of treasures and notes from friends. I think my parents bought the desk with the idea that I would do my homework on it. However, it was placed just outside my room in a dark hallway, and I never sat there to do my homework. The kitchen table upstairs had plenty of light, and I could socialize with Mom as dinner was cooking or gab with my friends on the phone while I worked on my homework. In *Reclaim Your*

Life, I shared that we all gravitate toward "centers of community." Usually, we don't like to be isolated for too long. This is especially true of children. Consider your children's ages and temperaments before you set up homework stations for them in their bedrooms. If they are always gravitating toward you, establish a homework center nearby. If they are in their late teens, they may want to move their homework back to their rooms, but I never did.

I recommend emptying your child's room of its contents and sorting each type of item. As you observe the kinds of things your children keep, their unique activity centers will emerge. You may find a lot of weights and exercise supplies in your teenage boy's room. Perhaps he needs a workout center established if you can carve out the space inside his room. You may discover a bevy of dolls spread all over your six-year-old's room, and she may need your help to create a special area for her dolls to congregate. Centers will naturally develop in your children's rooms based on their ages and tastes. Some kids love to read, and they want to store their precious books nearby, so a miniature library center might develop in their bedroom. Others love music and may need a special zone—complete with bean bags—for storing and listening to tunes.

Store and Display

Your children need appropriate furniture and products to store their belongings just as you do for yours. I recommend waiting to buy anything until you know exactly what you want to store. For example, don't buy desks for your children until you know they will actually do homework there. Otherwise the surface will get loaded with other things. Don't buy a set of furniture just because it goes together until you are sure you need each piece. Resisting these impulse purchases will save you money and will prevent creeping clutter. The more space we have to fill, the more likely we will be to fill it.

This principle also applies to those darling little containers that are so hard to resist, especially when they're on sale. I call this organizing shortcut the Product Panacea, where we mistakenly believe that the product is the answer to our organizing problems. Instead, the *process* is the answer. I advise bringing the right product into your space at the right time in the process. If you buy products prematurely, you won't know if they are the right products to suit your needs. Only when you see 20 dolls will you know how big a cradle you should purchase to store the dolls together. Only when you see 48 plastic horses will you know that you'll need a bookshelf or huge bin to store them instead of the cute basket you had in mind. Sort the belongings before you part with your money!

Children of all ages also need space to display their treasures in their bedrooms. Stuffed animals, figurines, models, trophies, and special collections should be stored by frequency of use. My favorite stuffed animals slept on my bed with me when I was little (well, maybe all the way through college), but my less special furry friends were displayed on a bookshelf.

Figurines and models and trophies are not handled very often, so they can be stored in a less accessible location. I like installing a high shelf around a child's bedroom, about 12 to 18 inches from the ceiling, judging by the tallest item you want to store. Mount the shelf with brackets, and you have a perfect spot to display your child's treasures while reclaiming floor and surface space for more frequently used items.

The goal of organizing children's bedrooms with them is to teach self-management. In other words, don't tidy their room for them while they are gone. That puts the responsibility for the child's state of order on your shoulders. It also robs the child of an important opportunity to learn life lessons like organizing, boundaries, and self-discipline. Recruit your children to help (yes, it is possible!), draw out their interests, establish activity centers around their unique needs, and implement storage and display choices once you know the items that need to be stored.

Guest Bedrooms

Once every year or two my cousins come to visit. Every time they come, I shuffle the contents of my upstairs to create a guest room for them. I want them to be comfortable and have room to put their suitcases out and hang things in a closet. I don't really have the space for a year-round guest room, but it really bothers me to have them stay on an air mattress. My compromise to not having a dedicated guest bedroom is to create one whenever they come.

Considerations

I really don't need a guest room if I get practical about it. No one else comes to visit and stay overnight. I need to use my bedrooms for other purposes, so why take up precious floor space with a bed that my dog would probably spend a lot of time enjoying? What about you? Do you really need a room for visitors? Can your friends and family stay on a pull-out couch elsewhere in the home? And let's be honest, if you have little kids running around, or teens making noise at all hours, would your guests prefer just to stay at a hotel?

By now you've probably determined if you truly need a guest room. If the answer is no, let it go and just create one like I do when you have guests. If you don't want to host company overnight, just send a nice gift basket to them at the local hotel. If the answer is yes, you'll have to carve out a space for overnight visitors.

Start by considering how much room you can spare. If you have an empty room you can dedicate as a guest space, fantastic! If not, you can conjoin a guest space with a hobby room, playroom, or even home office. If your multipurpose room is doubling as a guest space, however, be sure to think through the *primary* purpose that room is serving. Don't make your home office, for example, a guest space for frequent company if you need to be working late hours in your office.

Another consideration for creating guest space is whether you are hosting adults only or children as well. My brother and his wife can't stay at our home because we don't have all the space and equipment a toddler requires. My mom's house, on the other hand, has plenty of room, and Grandma has bought all the equipment her grandson might need!

When children move out, some people enjoy reclaiming their room as a guest space, yet you might want to think twice about this plan. Again, do you really need a guest room? If not, why not reclaim the space as an art studio or memorabilia room, or something in which you would find daily, practical enjoyment?

Needs and Nice-to-Haves

When you are organizing a guest space, all you really need is a bed, nightstand, alarm clock, and a little extra hanging and drawer space. The bed is the feature most dependent on space limitations. You can choose from hide-a-bed couches, futons, daybeds, or twin, full, queen, or king beds. If money isn't a consideration and space is limited, I like Murphy beds. Wall beds are so handy, they look attractive, and you can use the floor space for other things during the day.

If you can set up a dedicated guest room, you can think about additional features, such as an adjacent bathroom, a door for privacy, a special dresser, and even a suitcase rack. Your guest bedroom can be as simple or as elaborate as you like. Most people I work with don't have the luxury of a special room designated for guests, so we are often navigating the challenge of combining two or three purposes in one room.

Whatever bedroom you are organizing, focus on its inhabitants. Good organizing centers around the people who use the space. When you take the time to restore order to your bedrooms, you create respite from this busy world and infuse more harmony into your household!

10
The Bathroom

BATHROOMS ARE SPACES WE USE multiple times a day, yet they often receive little attention when we set out to organize our homes. We often neglect the bathroom, like other private spaces, precisely because it is so private. Having disorganized public spaces can be painfully embarrassing because other people see our chaos. But we reason that no one else will see our bathrooms, so we don't care how they look. We simply shut the door on our mess and hope no one ventures in.

You might be surprised how quickly you can completely organize your bathroom. Most bathroom projects our professional organizers have tackled have taken only four to six hours. Bathrooms are generally small and contain fewer items than many other rooms of our homes, so their contents can be removed and sorted in short order. If you can spare a half day without interruption, you can restore order to your master, children's, or other bathroom.

Master Bathroom

Tracey's master bathroom was a wasteland of forgotten products, plastic bags, and jumbled tools. Her under-sink cabinets hid a teetering pile of bottles and cleaning supplies. Inside her deep drawers were more hairbrushes than two people needed, washcloths, Band-Aids, nail polish, deodorant, and a mishmash of other toiletries. Each drawer held a varied collection of items, so whenever Tracey and her husband,

Jeff, wanted to find something, they had to go digging. Tracey was tired of it; she wanted a spa-like feeling when she walked into her room. She enlisted our help to tackle her challenge.

We began by emptying all the contents of Tracey's surfaces, cabinets, and drawers into boxes. Most of the categories that emerged were pretty common for bathrooms: skin care, hair care, nails, beauty-makeup, hygiene, mouth care, and first aid. Every time we found a new item, we looked at our boxes to see if we had already established a fitting category. If not, we asked, "What kind of product is this?" and began a new box of related items. The shaving cream ended up going in the skin care box, but some people have so much skin care that they prefer a separate shaving category.

In the sorting process, we discovered that Tracey had a unique Gifts category as well. Her mother often gave her gifts related to personal care, like miniature nail kits and matching sets of scented body care products. Most of them were still wrapped in cellophane or nested in baskets, and all of them were collecting dust. Tracey simply didn't take the time to unwrap these gifts and didn't find them useful, so she stashed the gifts into the dark corners of her bathroom cabinets. We started a box called Gifts. As we examined each one, we found some of the fruity scents had begun to ferment, and most of them could simply be tossed. In hopes of putting an end to the influx of neglected bath-related gifts, we recommended to Tracey that she ask her mom for gift certificates to her favorite stores!

His and Hers Space

Tracey and Jeff had only three drawers in the center of their cabinetry. They spent a lot of time pawing through the contents to find desired items. After we categorized everything, we talked further about their habits. From that conversation emerged Tracey's desire to have her own dedicated storage. She really wanted drawer space that was all hers, space that was protected from Jeff's wet toothbrush and razor. She was willing to take any drawer; she just wanted her own.

We decided that their *daily use* drawers would be reserved for the supplies they use the most. We designated the top drawer as Jeff's. Into it went his mouth care supplies, comb, deodorant, shaving supplies, and other daily use items. Tracey's drawer was the bigger of the two and held a fresh stack of washcloths, her hairbrush, mouth care supplies, and other frequently accessed items. Creating separate his-and-hers daily use drawers can prevent arguments!

Storage Considerations

In addition to creating his-and-hers drawers, we began to examine the remaining storage options and the categories of items left over. Peering into our boxes, we could estimate the amount of space we needed for each kind of item. Tracey had all the gear for manicures and pedicures, so we needed a fairly big spot to store the nail care supplies. Jeff loved to shop at the warehouse stores, like most of us, and he had accumulated about a dozen deodorant sticks, shampoos, and hair gels, so we knew we needed some decent real estate for warehouse overage. Extra mouth care supplies like toothpaste, floss, whiteners, and mouthwash, however, made up a much smaller category, so we realized we would only need a small bin to contain those items. When we knew the available space and the quantity of products to store, we took Tracey shopping for the appropriate containers. Too often, people make the mistake of buying products too early in the process and get bins that don't work because they're the wrong size.

The space under the sinks was deep and dark, yet we knew we had to maximize it to make room for all their goods. For this I like to use narrow plastic stacking drawers. They work beautifully under sinks when you have to make the most of vertical space but are dealing with the sink pipes in the middle of the space. They usually come in two- or three-drawer combinations, and the bottom drawer is larger than the top drawer(s). Tracey picked up four stacking drawer sets, and we set one on either side of the sink pipes in each of the under-sink cabinets. Mouth care and skin care supplies went in the top drawers, and we stored hygiene and first aid items in the larger bottom drawers.

As basic as it seems, we also put garbage cans on either side of the room. We found that Tracey had been opening packs of shampoo and deodorant and just stashing the plastic and cardboard packaging into the open spaces of her cabinets. She was amazed by how much real estate we reclaimed by simply purging her space of garbage!

Bathrooms are one of the more self-explanatory spaces to organize within the home. Be sure after you empty the space to wipe down all surfaces, removing the drawers and vacuuming or shaking out their contents if necessary. Beginning again with a clean slate is so refreshing. My advice for organizing your master bathroom is to let your categories develop by grouping your items together, purchase the right product at the right time in the process to contain the quantity of items you keep, and play defense by using his-and-hers drawers and garbage cans to eliminate bad habits. Once you have a clean and organized bathroom you can add personal touches like plants or decor that reflect your tastes. Reward yourself for an organizing process well done by decorating and settling into your own private spa, beach retreat, or whatever theme suits your fancy.

Children's Bathroom

After you've gone through the bathroom organizing process in an adult space, you can move on to your children's bathroom. When you gut their bathroom of all unnecessary stuff and set it up in an easy-to-use manner, you empower your kids to be more independent and to learn self-management skills.

You can follow the same discovery process of category development that you used in your bathroom to help your children create individualized systems for themselves. Giving each child his or her own daily use drawer (and subdividing the drawers into more finite categories where appropriate) will limit quarrels. Often, children have less gear than adults—that is, until they reach their teen years! While your children are still small, you can store extra towels or warehouse supplies in their cabinets if you find extra space.

You definitely want to keep a few things out of children's bathrooms altogether. Medicines, supplements, first aid, razors or other sharp implements, and cleaning supplies are not kid-friendly. I recommend that you pull those out of your children's bathrooms in the categorizing process even if you have the storage space.

Adults are more likely than children to fold their use-again towels, so one strategy our organizers use is to install hooks on the wall or even behind the door for kids to hang their towels. The only downside of using hooks is that towels with a heavy thread count don't always dry as thoroughly on hooks as they might on a rod. Purchasing color-coded towels for each child is a great idea that also helps with laundry and knowing which child left his wet towel on the floor! One of my clients has even had her children's names embroidered on their towels to ensure each child uses and maintains his or her own towel. Toothbrushing and hand washing are much splashier tasks for children than for adults, so keep at least one hand towel close to each sink in your children's bathroom.

Step stools are useful tools in children's bathrooms. Be sure to get one with skid-proof steps and feet. Another handy strategy is color-coding the bins you choose for each of their daily-use items or personal items in the shower. Correlate their colors to their towel colors if you can. The more you can help your children know which belongings are theirs and help them to use them and put them away properly, the better you are equipping them to be responsible for their own stuff in the adult world.

To enhance the organization you've established for your children, you can create and post a checklist to help them through their morning and evening routine. Young children might have to be reminded about brushing their teeth and washing their hands. Preteens might need a gentle cue to apply their new deodorant. Even older teens can benefit from being reminded about plucking their towels off the floor and wiping down the counters.

Additional Bathrooms

If you have an extra full-size bathroom that boasts under-sink cabinetry, you have some extra storage you can utilize. Begin by storing only bathroom-related items. If you need additional storage for warehouse purchases, like the 24-pack of toilet paper or the monstrous box of cotton balls, this cabinetry might be the perfect place.

If you don't need any more room for bathroom items in your extra bathroom, consider next the humidity and cleanliness of the bathroom. It's never a good idea to store food, medicines, vitamins, or other sensitive items in any bathroom, even if they are behind closed doors or drawers. Also, think about the purpose and location of this space when deciding what you should store inside. One of my clients uses the tub in her spare bathroom to wash her small dog. Accordingly she stores her pet's bathing supplies under the sink. If your extra bathroom is located near an overflowing linen closet, perhaps your beach towels can live in the under-sink cabinet while your bed linens remain in the hall closet.

Storage Strategies

Whatever bathroom you are organizing, keep in mind cabinet or drawer depth. Containers that reach all the way to the back of the cabinet or drawer make the most of your available real estate. On the other hand, if you have a shelf that is so deep you must layer your products, you can always store smaller items in a bin in front of the large, easy-to-see items at the back. If I am stuck with this situation, I will often put a label on the shelf itself stating the contents at the back of the shelf like Extra Shampoo and label the small bin in front

Hair Gel if that's what it contains. This way, I don't lose track of the items that had to be pushed to the back.

Another strategy I use is to create smaller categories for a large, unruly category. If I am dealing with a whole shelf of hair-care products, for example, I might label separate bins for hair gels, hair accessories, hair sprays, and brushes and combs. This way, I can subdivide a larger category into smaller subcategories and help clients know what they have and when they need to purchase more.

When you use bins or baskets to group bathroom items together, your belongings will stay clean. Removing items from a drawer or shelf is easy when you can remove them all at once. Then you can wipe out the drawer or shelf under the bin(s) to keep the surfaces clean. You can also occasionally empty a bin and wash down the bin itself with warm soapy water so that your supplies don't float around in dust bunnies and mysterious hair.

Some people use customized drawer sections to make use of every inch of drawer space. This product is also often used in kitchens to maximize gadget and utensil drawers. The plastic pieces fit together to form walls between your items. The advantage of this product is that you get to claim every bit of real estate for use. The downside of this product, however, is that you have to remove individual items from each section to clean the drawer. The upside of reclaimed space might, however, be worth it to you.

Organizing products stored on counters is another challenge. In general, your surfaces are easier to clean and nicer to look at if you can put all your products away behind closed doors. However, some people just don't have the space to store much, and others forget about their products if they are hidden away. For either case, I recommend using (and frequently wiping down) trays to separate and store like items. You can utilize bamboo trays, metal trays, or whatever fits your decor, but remember not to purchase anything until you know the quantity of what you need to keep on hand.

In my master bathroom, I have no storage in the tiny room that my shower and toilet share. The toilet paper and tissue were always running out in this highly trafficked room, and I knew I needed storage for extra paper goods, but I have only about 12 inches of space on either side of the toilet. Therefore, a free-standing cabinet was out of the question. I searched until I found a cute mirrored cabinet, which Trevor hung over the toilet. Now, it houses additional TP and Kleenex, and I'm happy I don't have to constantly replenish my paper goods supply from the laundry room. If you too are slim on space, don't forget that wall-mounted cabinets can provide much-needed storage. Again, wait until you know exactly what you want to store and how much space those items will consume before you buy something.

Another common category of items people store in bathrooms is travel paraphernalia. These items are best kept separate from other personal products since they are used a lot less frequently. I keep a few too many travel bags. I tell myself that each trip requires a different kind of bag, but I generally use the same ones over and over again. I actually don't really like any of the bags I have and probably just need to pitch them and start over. Trevor, on the other hand, grins from ear to ear as I busily pack my array of beauty and hair and shower supplies in various bags, and he drops his toothbrush, toothpaste, and deodorant into a large Ziploc bag! Since I travel a lot, I keep one primary travel bag packed and ready to go. If you are not a frequent traveler, I don't recommend this plan because it takes up more space, and items get old and forgotten.

Do you have a weakness for hotel samples? If so, do you actually use them? Or are you saving them for guests that never come? Tiny hotel shampoos, conditioners, soaps, lotions, mouthwashes, and sewing kits have a way of multiplying! I recommend that you donate your supply to your local homeless mission or women's shelter if you don't use them. You will enjoy reclaiming the space for other things. If you use them, or want to start using them, begin by placing one or two sets in your shower and daily use drawer.

Organizing the bathrooms in your household is not very time-consuming, and if you follow these processes and strategies, you can enhance the daily enjoyment of your home. Once you set up your private bath spaces for optimal use and streamline your storage, you will also have less conflict among family members as each person learns and practices better self-management. Remember, having a picture-perfect bathroom is not your goal. You want to create a space that works for you so you can move on with your priorities!

11

The Laundry or Utility Room

THE LAUNDRY ROOM IS ONE OF THOSE private spaces in the home that seems to draw in all kinds of unrelated items. It is a common dumping ground for dirty laundry, forgotten pocketed treasures, items that need to find a new home, overflow storage, and things you're trying to put out of sight. It can also serve as a pet area. Because of the typical vinyl flooring, some people put their kitty litter box inside the laundry room, and others use it as a holding pen for their unruly dogs. Depending on its size and location in the home, the laundry room can grow to include many other roles, including utility room, mudroom, or even hobby room.

Whether your room serves only the purpose of laundry central, or it doubles and triples as other purposes, your family needs easy access to it. In order to limit the time you spend in this space you may need to reorganize your existing room or, if you are lucky, add on a new space that better serves your needs. Most of us must make do with the space we have, so I've included in this chapter a lot of strategies I've used with my clients to help them create a laundry or utility room that works for their family.

Essentials and Nice-to-Haves

Few items are truly necessary in a laundry room. If you think about it, all you really need to accomplish the task is two appliances:

a washer and a dryer. You will want appropriate, easy to clean, waterproof flooring and (ideally) a drain in case of washer overflow. Some storage (or at least a shelf) for your laundry soaps and supplies is important. A garbage can to capture lint, dust bunnies, and dryer sheets is also a must.

Beyond the essentials, many other features can enhance your laundry experience. If at all possible, include a sink for soaking out stains, washing delicates, and drip-drying. An over-the-sink bar for drying items and storing hangars is also a plus. Drying racks, whether wall-mounted or free-standing, are useful. My grandparents' bathroom shower was the place that nylons and delicates were dried, and that seemed normal to me. Those of us who have no counter space for folding clothes often envy those who do, yet many who have that surface space end up dumping other things on the open counter instead and continue their habit of folding on a bed or couch. Additional storage like cabinets and drawers are nice-to-have features that expand the possibilities of your space. Many add-on features are available for the laundry room, but as you can see, we all operate a little differently in our own homes, and those habits must be taken into consideration.

If you are building a home or remodeling your existing home, the laundry room is one of the most important spaces to take the time to get right. We spend so much time on this household chore, why not make it as pleasant an experience as possible? When designing a new space, room layout depends on the limitations and purposes of the room. For example, homeowners will have less flexibility in layout if they have a tiny six-foot by six-foot space. The primary concerns would be accommodating ingress, egress, and the opening and closing of washer and dryer doors. Everything else, like shelving, hanging space, and a utility sink, is added after the primary needs are met. On the other hand, if the homeowner has generous square footage to work with, room layout can be as creative as the designer. Extras like folding space, built-in laundry baskets, countertop space for projects or crafts, and custom drawers and cabinets can be added as space allows.

Consider user habits when planning the use of space. Why go to the expense of built-in laundry baskets if family members use individual hampers in their bedrooms? Why build in two banks of drawers if the family keeps most utility items in the garage? If folding is most likely going to be done on your bedroom floor, why install lots of counter space for folding? Conversely, if habits need to change, go ahead and build in counter space for folding, but wall-mount a small television or stereo in the laundry room for entertainment to ensure that you actually stay in the space and use it as it was intended!

If you are starting from scratch, built-in storage is the most practical shelving for laundry and utility rooms because it maximizes the use of space. Built-in wall cabinets or open wall shelves optimize vertical space, which is important for a room that may be serving multiple purposes. Use cabinets to reduce a cluttered look. For very visual people, use open shelving to keep your supplies in view. If your laundry room is doubling as a utility room, built-in drawers are handy for organizing small utility items like batteries, cords, flashlights, tools, and hardware. Containing these items on shelves would require bins or baskets to store small parts.

When designing shelving, determine optimal depth of shelves by noting probable contents. Shelves should be deep enough to hold a large bleach jug, for example, but not so deep that items get hidden and lost or forgotten. Wherever possible, use adjustable shelving. Needs change over time, and flexibility is the goal in a utilitarian space.

Processing Considerations

Now that you've examined the necessary items and the setup of your laundry room, you'll want to consider how you actually process laundry. If you've read *Reclaim Your Life,* you probably remember that Trevor and I have an ongoing laundry war. He thinks the floor was specially designed to store his shoes, slippers, belts, coats, and dirty laundry. He doesn't even mind storing dress clothes he plans on wearing again in a pile with filthy work clothes. We've tried (I've tried) everything possible to capture his laundry effectively. From placing a basket at the end of the bed to using a canvas hamper with no lid, my laundry storage solutions only go as far as his desire to move his dirty clothes out of the way. The canvas hamper works for a while until he feels like rebelling, and then the floor becomes a wading pool of clothes. I guess in the grand scheme of ways to rebel, laundry is pretty minor. If there's a laundry war at your house too, I hope these next few process steps will be helpful to you.

Capturing the laundry is the first step to processing it. If you have children (or spouses) who can tell dirty from clean laundry, you can usually recruit them to capture it in one location, either inside their bedrooms or direct-deposit into a basket in the laundry room if it's nearby.

Since my laundry room is next to my master bedroom, I like to simply drop my dirty clothes into a basket right in the laundry room. That way, my clothes don't get mixed into a stagnating hamper in the bedroom. Once my baskets are full, I do a load of towels and sheets or whites or darks, and I keep up with laundry just fine. This way, if Trevor's laundry is taking over the bedroom floor, I can at least keep my laundry going and let him deal with his.

Sorting the laundry is the next step in processing it. I make sorting a natural part of capturing by keeping three laundry baskets set up on top of my washer and dryer at all times: one basket each for whites, lights, and darks. You can use individual three-section hampers inside each person's bedroom to combine the capture and sorting process in your bedrooms as well. Otherwise, you can choose to haul all the hampers or baskets into the hall or laundry room at once, and sort into piles from there. You'll also want to determine who is responsible to sort laundry. I like making the capture and sort process a one-two punch so that it happens at the same time, so whoever is capturing is also sorting. If your children are very young or if you are the designated launderer, you can decide how you want to sort.

Drying clothes is the next processing step you'll need to organize. If you have limited space, you can simply drip dry items in the shower or over the tub. If you have enough space in your laundry room, you can install a bar or rack on the wall to dry delicates. I use a rolling garment rack in my small laundry room. I divide the bar into the following categories: Dry (for damp clothes), Put Away (dry cleaning), Steam, and Defuzz. This makes it so easy to stage my clothes on hangers.

One of the best gifts I ever received (as far as corded appliances go) was a professional steamer. I use it all the time to remove wrinkles from my clothes. I hate to iron, so I either send clothes to the dry cleaner (I use the door-to-door service so I never have to leave my house) or steam them. If they have to be ironed, off they go to the cleaners. My time is valuable, and ironing is not how I want to spend it. If you steam, be sure you have a vent to move the humid air out of your room; otherwise, the water may damage your walls. If you iron, God bless you. My mom irons in front of the television. If you iron in the laundry room, install a wall-mounted television or at least a radio to provide you with some company.

The last consideration of laundry processing is disseminating clean laundry. This is about as exciting as putting away clean dishes from the dishwasher. No one wants to do it. Again, you must determine a distribution system and who is responsible for this task. One of my clients designates a colored basket for each of her children. She washes, dries, and folds the clothes and then loads the clean clothes into her children's color-coded baskets. Once the green basket is full, her son Tommy had better put away his clothes. If he doesn't and his clean clothes sit there all week, no more laundry will be done for Tommy. I like that system because it helps children to self-manage. Other (tired and sometimes resentful) moms shoulder all the responsibility for laundry, from capturing to sorting to drying and folding to ironing and distributing. In my opinion, the earlier you recruit your children and spouse to help, the more you will be communicating to everyone that the home belongs to everyone, not just Mom.

More Space, More Purposes

Some folks have a laundry room that could be featured in a magazine with lovely windows, built-in sorting baskets, and ample counter space. Others cope with a laundry closet in the middle of a hallway or a laundry corner in a cold garage or basement. If your laundry space is basically a nook in a hallway, complete with bifold doors, you are probably used to folding clothes on the floor and dealing with traffic flow problems. Whatever your space is like, you probably want to maximize it so you can minimize the time and angst you expend on this household chore. The larger the room you have to work with, the more possibilities you have to store more types of items.

The stuff that should go in your laundry room is determined by your available space and how your family uses the room. If your laundry room is a dumping ground, I would pull everything out of the space and assess the quantity of each item you store inside. You might be surprised by the wide variety of random items you find. When I work with clients, I want to know how much their inventory varies from month to month. In other words, if they have 12 rolls of toilet paper stored in the laundry room, is that normal? Do they usually have less or more? Assessing quantity and inventory are essential first steps to know what you actually have and how much of it you have crammed in your laundry space so that you know how much space to allocate to each category of item.

Since your laundry room must first serve its namesake, you must make room for a washer and dryer, laundry baskets or bins, detergents and bleach, spot removers, and dryer sheets. Equipment like drying racks, a dry cleaning bin or bag, an iron, an ironing board, and maybe a steamer will need to find a home as well. Hangars, clothes pins, and other incidentals will also be stored inside. One of my clients taught me her trick of creating a sock orphanage in a basket on the counter. I love this idea because long-lost socks can be reunited if they ever appear from the corners of your sheets.

If you store all the laundry items here and still have more real estate, the next thing I would add is cleaning supplies. Window, floor, surface, and furniture cleaners must find a destination. I like storing the different kinds of cleaners in separate bins so I can easily remove the bin from the shelf, see with one glance what is inside, and become aware when I need to buy more. Rags, mops, brooms, and the vacuum usually reside in the laundry room as well.

After you've designated your laundry room for laundry and cleaning, if you have more space, you can add additional purposes. Often, laundry rooms become utility rooms as lightbulbs, batteries, picture hooks, flashlights, electrical cords and extenders, a set of tools, hardware, and furniture repair items are added. Overflow paper goods like trash bags, toilet paper, and tissue also frequently find their way into this space. When I'm organizing, I also find household goods like candles and seasonal decor located in this room.

I've seen a host of other categories in laundry or utility rooms, including pet supplies, gift wrap, and hobbies. We store our dog's towels in our laundry room. Many people also store their pet shampoos, brushes, tools, and sometimes even their food in this space. A utility room might also be a gift-wrap center, complete with wrap, bags, bows, ribbons, and cards. Some of our clients with small children dedicate a cabinet or two in their utility room for arts and crafts, especially for those messy paints, glitters, and glues. For one of my clients, we even set up a child-sized table and chairs in the middle of her spacious utility room so that her kids could work on their projects over the easy-to-clean vinyl floor. The number and type of categories of items you can store in your utility room will be determined by your available space.

Proximity to Other Rooms

One of the best factors you can use to determine how you should organize your laundry room is its proximity to other rooms. My laundry room is upstairs, next to my laundry-producing bedrooms. When the rooms are that close, we can easily direct deposit our dirty clothes right into the room itself. I also have the benefit of not having to lug baskets and hampers downstairs to another location to do the laundry. Proximity to bedrooms has given us (okay, me) the freedom to capture and sort dirty clothes practically at the point of use.

If your laundry room is adjacent to the garage or has exterior access it will often serve as a mudroom. Family members piling out of the car or coming in from the rain will likely drop their shoes, coats, hats, and bags in the mudroom space. Hooks and bins to capture those items would be appropriate. Likewise, if your utility room has an exterior entrance, adults may download whatever is in their arms, like mail and groceries. Many men with whom I've worked find that this is also the spot they unload change, business cards, and other collected paraphernalia from their pockets. If your laundry room has become a landing spot, you must implement systems (like a Go Elsewhere basket or a "deal with by the end of every week" tray) to move those items on to their destination.

Exterior access from your utility room also makes it an ideal launching pad. If you run in the mornings, you may want to store your portable music player and its charger here. Cell phones and portable electronic devices can be charged here and retrieved daily before work. If you live near a community pool, or have a pool yourself, you may store towels and suntan lotion in this room for easy access.

If your laundry or utility room is near the kitchen, and if you have additional space, you can store overflow kitchen items like infrequently used appliances, picnic ware, nonperishable foods, or table decor and linens. As I mentioned before, since the kitchen table is a magnet for children and their art projects, the laundry room may serve as an ideal spot to store craft supplies nearby. Let proximity to other rooms guide the unique contents of this room.

Creative Storage

Honestly, I have never seen one laundry room exactly like another in the homes I've been inside. Everyone must determine the available space, start by adding the most important functions and their related supplies first, and then add in additional categories based on how they use their home. There are no rules!

Well, perhaps I do have one rule: For your own sake, try to make the laundry room a pleasant place! Please, we are in the laundry room more than we would like. Laundry is a chore we can't avoid unless we have a maid. So I say make it a fun space that you like to be in! Creative storage options can add so much to a room that can otherwise be dull, poorly lighted, and depressing. Below are some of my ideas to help you maximize and personalize your storage. Remember, good organizing is customized to your unique lifestyle and personality, so if these ideas I've used for myself and clients don't work for you, pitch them and create your own!

- Free-standing storage, including industrial post shelving, self-assembled bookshelf units, and modular stacking storage, can add additional options for stowing laundry or utility goods.

- Old-fashioned railroad cars employed hat racks that also offered a bar for hanging coats. Mount one of these beauties on an unused wall, and you'll have room for hangars, hanging items, and folded items.

- Braced shelving around the perimeter of the room, mounted 12 to 18 inches from the ceiling, can provide additional storage for infrequently used items or decorative display. You can find unique brackets at hardware or salvage stores.

- The space over a window is often overlooked. Mounting a shelf above this space can add storage space for a variety of objects or a decorative collection.

- Wall-mounted shadow boxes or miniature shelves or drawers offer accessible storage for small items, like hardware or craft supplies.

- Dead space over and under the utility sink can be put to many uses. Mount a paper towel rack or hand towel bar over the sink for drying hands. Install a pull-out garbage can or some shelving to maximize space under the sink. (Measure first, since the pipes can pose a challenge.) Alternatively, many plastic bins with removable drawers are narrow enough to fit on either side of pipes.

- The narrow wall space above the washer and dryer but under wall-mounted cabinets is often neglected. Hang accordion style hooks on the wall for drying delicates. That's what I do since I have limited drying space. Beware that items don't fall behind the appliances though!

- Behind-the-door inches can go a long way to optimize storage. I use two plastic coat hooks hung over the back of the door to brace an ironing board. Or install low-profile hooks on the wall behind the door to store and hide mops and brooms.

- Don't forget the space above wall cabinets for display or storage space. I use mine to display vintage soap boxes.

- I use an old-fashioned metal milk jug for storing my laundry detergent. I buy the economy size detergent at the warehouse store and transfer the soap to the jug. I use a vintage metal scoop to measure the detergent.

- Instead of boring plastic containers, look for unique bins and baskets that reflect your style. Remember, don't buy products too early in the organizing process. Only buy what you need when you know exactly what you need to store!

- I like using plant baskets (you can find a surprising array at local stores) for storing cleaning supplies because they are lined in plastic for easy wiping.

- Metal buckets, cans, and bins can be recycled into utility room staples. Buckets are great for soap and scrubbers. Cans are wonderful homes for pens, scissors, and tools. Bins can be stacked for recycling or used for separating hobby parts or art and craft supplies.

- Wall mount narrow dowels for ribbon spool holders, and use tall buckets or baskets for storing gift wrap rolls upright.

I have to admit that I felt a little like "Ask Heloise" writing this chapter. Organizing a laundry room can easily feel like a "happy homemaker" task, which is exactly how I don't want it to seem. Having an orderly utility room isn't about making sure your sheets are folded perfectly and scented with linen spray, or creating a designer room complete with cute decor. It isn't about how I organize mine or how your neighbors organize theirs. It isn't about being a decorating genius; it's about finding what works for you. Your laundry or utility room is no different from the rest of your household; you designate its purpose according to the way *your family* uses your home.

My best advice to you if you want to organize your laundry or utility room is to enlist your family's help as early as possible. This is a room that everyone needs, uses, and benefits from, so everyone should participate. One of my clients stated, "Organizing our laundry room helped everyone take ownership and step up to the plate." My wish for you is that your laundry or utility room can become a pleasant place in which your tasks are streamlined so you can get in, get out, and move on with the business of living!

12

The Home Office

IF YOUR HOME OFFICE LOOKS LIKE it was struck by a hurricane, you are not alone! The number one request we get at our organizing company is to restore order to the home office. From paper piles to nomadic items floating around, no one seems to know what to do with this frustrating space.

Some people have a dedicated room for this purpose, and others have a desk tucked inside another space, like the kitchen, bonus room, or playroom. Some folks call their home office a den, others dub it the study, and others just refer to it as the office. Whatever you call your space, the home office is the personal business center of the household, and you should give it careful attention to ensure proper functioning.

If you have ever thought about hiring a professional organizer to help you in your home and your budget is limited, apply an expert's help in this room first. The home office is the most important place to start because as our lives become more complicated, so do our systems. The home office is one of the more complex spaces in the home to organize successfully because of the many activities, roles, and preferences to take into consideration. In my observation, the home office is the one space that will give you the most peace of mind once it is organized. For me to limit a discussion about home offices to a single chapter is difficult. It is such an important space; I could write a whole book about home offices!

Dealing with Incoming Paper

One cannot consider home offices independent of the proliferation of paper delivered to your door every day. The first means of self-defense to protect your home office from sure burial is to capture the mail appropriately. In our household, Trevor loves to get the mail. He takes our dog out to the box, and they gather the mail and bring it into the kitchen. He opens his pay stub weekly and snags his aviation magazines. From there, I open the mail, recycling and shredding most of it.

The items that remain must be paid, filled out, filed, or given some other type of attention. I call these "actionable" items. Actionable items form the tasks that you are responsible for in your home office. From insurance paperwork you must fill out and submit for reimbursement, to bills to pay, to periodicals to review, actionable items must reach the business center of your home. If the person who retrieves the mail deposits it randomly throughout the house or sneaks some of it off to an unknown location, proper routing is thwarted from the get-go.

We also bring paper into our homes in our briefcases and handbags and add to the flood of incoming documents. If that's not enough, many of us love having a hard copy of documents, so we constantly hit "print" on our computers and thereby unwittingly contribute to the volume of paper in our households. Being aware of the various means by which paper seeps into your home can help you route it properly.

Routing by Processing Location

Most of us have never thought through which activities should be taking place in which spaces in our homes, especially dealing with paper and office items. One of the first questions you will want to answer about each room is this: What should be happening in this space? Many of us bring mail into the kitchen and stack papers to be filed on the stairs or on some other surface. Since paper tends to travel throughout the house, the initial step in organizing your home office is deciding which processing activities you want to happen in which locations.

You might decide that you want to capture mail on the kitchen counter and immediately sort out the pieces to toss, recycle, or shred. Then, if you have a household hub, which we discussed in chapter 4, you might move the remaining mail that requires action onto the hub. If you don't have a hub or have designated it for other purposes, you may need to figure out a method to move your actionable items into the home office. Alternatively, you may decide that you want all incoming mail and paperwork to go directly to the office so you don't have to trace its course throughout the home. You must make these decisions according to how you actually use your home. If you have a chaotic kitchen, for example, you might not want it to serve as an initial landing spot for mail for fear that the mail might be lost.

Paper isn't the only thing that wanders all over the house; supplies tend to spread as well. If you find that office supplies (like paper, rulers, pens and pencils, mailing supplies, staplers, and file folders) are always hard to find, you will want to determine the primary point of use for those items. For example, your kids might use some school supplies in their homework area, but you may also want some of those same items stored in the home office. In addition, you may want an office-supply drawer in your kitchen or adjacent household hub as well. You could purchase a set of black tools (scissors, stapler, hole punch) for your office, a red set for the kids, and a blue set for the kitchen to eliminate confusion and borrowing. Limiting your office-related supplies to locations where you will process paper and accomplish work will help you declutter your home.

Routing by Job Description

Routing paper into its appropriate destination is a struggle for almost every client with whom I've ever worked. Many married couples divide the paperwork duties, and that division of labor can inform the routing process. By dividing duties, they have essentially created job descriptions for themselves. If the husband manages the finances, all paperwork related to banking, credit, expenses, investments, and taxes can go to his desk. If the wife manages all medical, household, personal, and school issues, then those types of paper can be routed to her desk.

Separate job descriptions merit separate workstations, just as in the professional environment. If spouses absolutely must share a desk (which is dangerous territory), I recommend two distinct areas to capture and process paper by whose role it fits into. If possible, I recommend establishing individualized stations—like his and hers offices or individual desks—for each person to tackle his or her projects. Can you tell I lean heavily toward separate desks for spouses? They can be marriage savers!

My friend Grace and her husband, Don, each have their own office. She says that one determining factor caused them to split off into two spaces: He is a slob. Don keeps all his paper in piles on any available surface and also on the floor. He never dusts his office, she thinks it looks like a junk heap. Grace is unmotivated when she works alongside her husband in the same space because of his mess. Creating two offices so he could hibernate in his space (which I guess is a job description of sorts) and she could work on household tasks in visual peace was the solution that worked for them.

Unfortunately, Grace found a downside to having separate spaces: All paper is supposed to be routed to her, but Don often hijacks it and holds it hostage in his office. Anything related to the computers, receipts for his purchases, or even automotive papers can disappear without a trace. Ruefully, Grace shared with me that last summer Don lifted from the mail papers from the DMV notifying them that their tags were due to be replaced. The deadline came and went, and soon they were the recipients of a $350 traffic ticket for expired plates! The moral of the story is this: Route by job description, and warn paper hijackers not to derail your system!

I also recommend routing completed work into a joint filing system, regardless of who manages which papers. Both spouses must understand the filing system so that either one can easily find financial, medical, household, or personal documents. Often people don't realize the importance of having a central, easily understood personal filing system until an emergency or a death in the family occurs.

What do you do if one person is not fulfilling his or her job description in the business of running your household? Well, if you were the boss, you could fire the person, but that doesn't tend to work well in families! If your spouse is supposed to be taking care of finances, for example, but the mail has been piling up for months and you are getting late fees, you'll need to have a frank conversation about options.

If you are willing to take over the financial role, that might be a solution, but believe it or not, relinquishing the task might be difficult for the delinquent spouse. I can only advise you to keep all conversations calm and mutually supportive. Focus on solutions, and keep blame out of the equation; this is about your peace of mind. If you are not willing to take over the financial role, perhaps you can hire a bookkeeper. If you would be willing to take it on but have too many other things on your plate, perhaps you could hire some part-time help with the other things. Shuffling job descriptions may be necessary to the proper functioning of your home office, which is the operations center of your home. I've seen many households experience backlog and gridlock due to neglected roles.

Distinguishing Personal and Professional Offices

Writing a chapter about home offices would be unfair without addressing folks who actually run their business from their house.

Those of us who run a home-based business or who frequently bring work home from the office experience the convergence of our personal and professional lives in one chaotic space. If you have an at-home business, you are likely operating out of your home office, or perhaps you are one of the lucky few who have two distinct spaces. I've seen both setups work successfully, so whichever arrangement you have, take the time now to consider some observations. Perhaps what I've observed in the trenches can help you reimagine and redefine your space.

Having two spaces and working in a combined space can each bring challenges. Few people have the luxury of having both a personal office and a dedicated business office within the home. The organic inseparability of personal and business life may even create an argument against two distinct spaces. Most of us can't turn on and turn off roles very easily, and if we have two offices, we are moving back and forth between and attempting to operate out of each. Also, if you have two offices you may lose track of information and duplicate supplies and equipment. On the other hand, the downsides of joining your professional and private lives in one single space include the likelihood of blurred boundaries, creeping clutter, and confusion.

The following considerations will help you assess whether to set up two offices with distinct purposes or one office that caters to both personal and professional needs.

Two Offices: Personal and Professional

If you think you want separate spaces for personal and business use, determine which activities would take place in each environment. I'm not referring to separate his and hers offices so each spouse can have sacred space; I'm talking about creating two unique spaces for different uses: one personal and one strictly professional.

For example, if you have a small desk space that adjoins the kitchen, you could outfit it with a laptop, files, calendar, supplies, and a paper-processing center to create a household hub. At this hub you can pay bills, make appointments, coordinate schedules, and sort mail. The spare room or office could then be dedicated as professional space for your business. If you have a large home with extra rooms, you can choose two different spaces and name one the home office and one the business. Alternatively, some larger homes are built with two office spaces that could provide ideal real estate for private and business use.

Two separate spaces often make more sense when the household has two adult members, one or both who work from home. The spouse who works from home may be keenly interested in creating a professional boundary. One of my clients actually built a shed-like structure onto his property to use as his professional space. He kissed his wife and kids goodbye every morning at the same time and reported to work in the yard! His building was outfitted with air conditioning and all the amenities of a professional office. He came home for lunch and at a prescribed time at night, but otherwise, he was considered away for the day. With this boundary established, his space was clearly defined, and he could fulfill his work role in this little shed. His wife then used their joint home office as the personal business center of the home. It was easy to route paper and items to either space: Any business items went to his shed, and any personal items went upstairs to the home office.

If you are a single person who wants to set up both personal and professional offices, you will want to designate the tasks that will take place in each space. You may find yourself shuttling between the two spaces and realize that your need to have designated professional space is less important if you are the only one puttering around the house. I recommend setting official office hours for anyone who wants to work from home. Instituting dedicated time to work in each location will preserve the effectiveness of both personal and professional offices.

One Office: Combining Worlds

If your home does not afford two likely office locations, or if you opt to conjoin your personal and business lives in one space, anticipate more activity and tasks taking place in that environment. To balance the two kinds of tasks in one room, start by making lists of the activities you will perform and the space you will need.

List all the personal tasks (like capturing mail, paying household bills, and coordinating a schedule) that will take place in the office. Do you have a laptop, or will you need a keyboard tray because you have a PC? Do you require the space to spread out and see all your work at once, or can you get away with a three- or four-foot work surface? Be sure you take into consideration your natural preferences.

Along with your proclivities, assess the amount of paper associated with the home duties, and dedicate commensurate storage and work space. As far as actionable paper goes, you'll need a bill-paying system, a center for processing incoming paper, and an area to store pending projects. Unless you store permanent paper elsewhere, your well-designed home filing system will probably require four small drawers or one lateral file cabinet. In addition to paper, you'll need storage for stuff. Most home offices I've seen need at least one or two banks of drawers and some cabinet space to store binders, extra reams of paper, and other supplies.

Next, evaluate your professional job description. What tasks do you perform on a daily basis? Are your tasks primarily executed electronically? Do you need surface space to assemble packets or place peripherals? Will prolific reference material require bookshelves? Do you need slots for literature and forms or drawers for office supplies? Most professionals who have an effective filing system need four to eight small file drawers or two lateral cabinets to store their permanent paper. Adequate filing space is essential in a home office to prevent the pileup of completed paper that needs a destination.

The downside of combining the personal and professional space may include a more crowded work space, the stress associated with prolific tasks, and the temptation to neglect necessary business-related work for personal projects. Most home-based business owners I work with operate in one single office, usually because of limited space. If you take the time to think through the tasks you will be performing and provide the necessary work and storage space, I believe you can function effectively in one space.

Setting Up the Home Office

Once you've decided whether you will use one or two spaces for your home office, you can turn your attention to setting up your space optimally. Every home office is unique. Properly planning the setup of your home office will prepare you to successfully execute the activities central to your personal and professional lives.

When our professional organizers finish organizing a home office for one of our clients, the relief is palpable. Think about it: When your ancient filing is finally taken care of, when your bills are finally up-to-date, and when no more scary unknowns (like collection notices or unsigned permission slips) are lurking in your piles, you feel in control, perhaps for the first time in a long time. An organized home office is an essential center of a functional household. You will liberate yourself by expending some energy on this space.

You may already have a home office that is working well for you, and in that case, my setup suggestions may simply affirm what you've already done. If, on the other hand, your home office is a source of frustration for you, this may be your opportunity to start over and establish a space that works for you. These four strategies will help ensure you've covered the scope of your home office needs.

1. Invest in Adequate Furniture

Many home offices look like college dorm rooms. Most of us just patch together a home office, snagging furniture from other rooms and cobbling together a collection of mismatched items rather than investing in the appropriate furniture. But improper furniture can in fact contribute to disorganization. If you are resisting purchasing a four-drawer file cabinet, for example, your two-drawer file cabinet will be bursting at the seams. Filing new documents will be nearly impossible because the file folders are jammed so close together in your overflowing drawers. Likewise, if you have not dedicated enough desk space, you might find your projects relocated to the floor. With a little detective work (like observing a jammed file cabinet or piles on the floor), you can note your habits in your space to discover which furniture is not working for you.

Every office needs ample, clear, work space, room for peripheral equipment and computer hardware, a spot for reference materials, file space, and a location for frequently referenced supplies and paper. Before you run out to purchase furniture, make sure you have taken the time to discover what you really need. I often see people purchase furniture for their home office prematurely. Something may look good or be on sale, but that doesn't mean you should make it yours!

When we added on to our home a space for my own home office, I spent days going over all the contents I wanted to store. Since I intended to fit the space with custom furniture, I had to know exactly how many file drawers and supply drawers I needed. I had to know how much cabinet space and flat storage I needed for the literature we disseminate. I measured my existing desk and considered carefully whether I would need more or less work surface.

If you are starting over or purchasing new furniture to contain paper and items, start by discovering how many drawers you will need by evaluating all the stuff you want to store, like technology supplies, mailing supplies, checks, stamps, disks, office supplies, notepads, and the like. Our organizers help people empty their office and categorize each type of item into separate boxes. Then we can visually tell whether they need a little storage (for 12 notepads) or a lot of storage (for 200 CDs) for each kind of item. Examine how many shelves you will need by assessing how many upright things you want to store, including reference material, books, magazines, binders, and so forth. Pull all your files out and put them into hanging files in bankers' boxes (which approximately equal the size of one small file drawer) so they move easily. This way, you can guesstimate how many file drawers you'll need. As you can see, choosing the right piece of furniture begins not with its looks but with its storage capacity and function.

2. Properly Place Equipment

Once you have purchased the right furniture, place peripherals and hardware by frequency of use. If the printer is used daily, it should be within reach. If the CPU is only accessed for troubleshooting, it can be placed under or next to the desk. Some people like to use a CPU trolley to lift their CPU off the ground to ensure more air flow. If you rarely use a scanner, you can place it outside the work area. Many scanners are now built in to printer-copier machines, so consider whether you can donate yours if you are planning on purchasing an all-in-one machine. Sometimes peripherals can only be located as far away as cords allow. When setting up hardware, be conscious of access to drives, trays, and cords. Do not block access to drawers or leg room with tangled cords.

3. Establish Centers

The efficient home office is zoned into at least these three activity areas: the work center (usually the desktop), the reference center, and the supply center. Of course, every home office will operate a little differently. Some people store very few supplies and can get away with one simple supply drawer. Other people store mountains of materials inside their cabinets and will require more space for supplies.

The work center should include clear work space, the computer, and accessible office supplies. This is where you will spread out your projects and get them done. At my desk I have within my easy reach my laptop, my PDA, my ten-key calculator, my stapler, all my office supplies stored in my Essentials Centers®, and all my current projects stored in my Project Centers®. (For more on Restoring Order® brand desktop organizing products, see the back pages of this book.) I set my work center up to store the files and supplies I use the most often.

The items in the reference center will vary from person to person but usually include binders, manuals, dictionary, and professional books and materials. Reference materials are commonly stored on bookshelves or in cabinets. My customized desk includes a pull-out shelf below the desktop that contains five reference binders I refer to daily.

A supply center could contain office and paper supplies inside a cabinet or within drawers. The key is to know what you want to contain. If you want to store pens, pencils, highlighters, and markers, you will probably want a drawer organizer within a drawer. If you want to store notepads, you could probably just stack them in a drawer or on a shelf in a cabinet, depending on frequency and point of use. Be sure to consider storage location along with access. I use paperclips daily, so they are in one of the Essentials Center drawers closest to me. However, I only have to fill my stapler with extra staples every month, so the extra box of staples is located in the farthest drawer.

4. Make Paper Work for You

I told you I could write a whole book about home offices! I'll close this chapter by mentioning the three most important paper-management systems. These essential systems must be established to tame the paper pileup and allow you to work on one thing at a time. Successful paper-management systems must include a way to process actionable paper, store projects, and access a customized permanent filing system.

Processing Paper

The first system you should establish is a processing center to capture and queue incoming paper for action. This is the single most important system in any home or office. Actionable paper is paper that represents something you need to do. It includes quick turnover items. Think of your processing center as a runway: You land and take off on a runway; you never park. The idea is to keep incoming paper moving through your processing center until you can either file it or dispose of it.

I recommend sorting incoming paper not by what it is (such as a medical or financial document) but instead by what you need to do with it. If you are looking at a bill for medical service, ask yourself what you need to do with it. The answer is that you need to pay it. So you will need a tray called To Pay in your processing system. If you are looking at your bank statement, ask what you need to do with it. You may need to reconcile it and then file it. If that's the case, you should put the bank statement in a tray that says To Reconcile, and after you've finished that task, you can move it onto a tray that says To File.

Your paper-based actions will be totally unique to you. Some people have a great filing system, so they file immediately. Therefore, they don't need a tray that says To File. Others make a lot of phone calls and might want a tray that says To Call. People who have a lot of things to do might want to separate a huge stack of items requiring follow-up into To-Do *A* and To-Do *B* or Immediate and Action.

Generally, trays work best for dividing your action-oriented paper. For this reason, I have created the Restoring Order Action Center®, a processing center that can be customized with trays and drawers to help people capture and take action on their paper. For more information about setting up a processing center that works for you, visit the Action Center page at www.ReclaimYourOffice.com.

Storing Projects

The next essential system you will need to manage paper in your home office is a way to store current and pending projects. Distinct from paper that needs to be processed, project-based paper is current or pending but has several steps or documents involved. I like to think of projects as short-term parking because they hang around for a while until they are complete.

For example, perhaps you are planning a party. You will likely have a guest list, a menu, information about entertainment, and other papers to put together into a file or sleeve so they are not separated. The party file has a shelf life because it has a timeline associated with it, and when it is completed, it will be retired. You may be accumulating paper for other projects, such as a household remodel or research for a new type of auto insurance.

Generally, people use a wire incline sorter to store their project file folders upright. These work for some people, and they are definitely an inexpensive option for keeping your projects in your view. The downside of these sorters is that papers tend to fall toward the middle or out the sides. I designed a Project Center to contain project files in a bleachered row. It has some important distinctions from the wire sorter. First, it is closed on the sides so files don't fall out or look messy. Second, it has removable dividers to make room for thick files. To learn more about options for vertical file storage for projects, visit the Project Center page at www.ReclaimYourOffice.com.

Permanent Files

Lastly, every home needs a good filing system. I call the documents in your file system your permanent papers because you intend to keep them for a long while. Think of this as long-term parking. Most people don't have a good filing system, and if you're one of those people, I recommend you gut what you have and start over.

Though many people organize files alphabetically, this can cause problems. You may decide something should go under *I* for Insurance, but when your spouse looks for the file (or even you at a later date) *H* for Homeowners Insurance might seem more sensible. Alphabetical systems only make sense in the moment, they are more prone to duplication, and when you are looking for a file you search your file drawer, you also have to remember how you labeled the file.

Instead, try grouping your files into major categories like financial, medical, household, and personal. Subcategorize each of these major categories as enough files of like kind emerge. For example, your financial category might be subcategorized into banking, credit, investments, and taxes. I use tab positions to indicate subcategory (for example, banking files might all be in left tab position, credit files might be in center tab position, and investment files might be in right tab position). Label the file folder tab to indicate the subcategory and file name. Then, assign a separate drawer to each category so you can keep your various kinds of files altogether.

Recently one of our organizers helped a client begin a file system. We were only a few appointments into the project when the mom was unexpectedly taken to the hospital for an illness. Because her teenage son had been observing our organizer help his mom file her medical paperwork, he could direct his dad to his mom's important records. Gutting your filing system (or creating one for the first time) can be a lifesaver!

Without proper paper management systems to anchor their home office, people struggle in a sea of confusion, ill-equipped to capture information and documents. Since those documents affect the proper functioning of your life and household, you will want to capture them and move them onto action.

The successful home office is a result of thoughtful assessment, space planning, and user-centered design. Whether you are running a household, a business, or both, investing in the process of organization will bring you more productivity, satisfaction, and freedom.

13

The Hobby Room

Susan led me down the hall, issuing many disclaimers as we made our way to her soon-to-be craft room. She explained that she hadn't completely moved into the room yet. Lots of boxes were littering the floor, she warned. I smiled and told Susan I would be okay with whatever we found. After all, she and her husband had just moved into this larger home, and now she finally had the space to create her long-awaited craft room.

When we arrived in the room, I found a few mismatched pieces of furniture, lots of tall moving boxes, a dusty collection of baskets of all sizes, and a huge old television sitting on the floor. It looked like the classic spare room. I pulled up the shade on the window to provide more light and took a seat on a stool. I invited Susan to tell me about what we would find in the boxes, and together we began to sift through them. Each supply we fished out of a box had an associated hobby. As each new item emerged, so did a story.

Some of the first items we found included heavy mat board and picture frames of all sizes and descriptions. Some of the frames had photos in them, and others still had the price tag on them. Susan explained that she intended to pull out the outdated family photos and replace them with new ones. Indeed, her grown daughters were caught in a time warp in these photos, frocked in their grade-school dresses with their hair parted down the middle. Now that Susan was a grandmother, she said she wanted to reuse some of those frames for pictures of her grandchildren. I asked her about the unused frames, and she said she had picked most of them up on sale and hoped to find photos to fit them. Picture framing went onto our list of hobbies that Susan could reclaim in this dedicated space.

Greeting cards by the hundreds began to appear as we continued unpacking. Construction paper for making greeting cards, envelopes, scored blank cards, stamps, stickers, decals, and even previously used cards also emerged. Boxed sets of greeting cards of all descriptions and individual cards with matching envelopes bought at a discount were all jumbled together. We began to sort them into categories: Sympathy, Birthday, Christmas. As we pored over the cards and embellishments, Susan told me she hates paying full price for cards. She loves the satisfaction she gets when she gives handmade cards to friends or family. We added Susan's enthusiasm for cost-effective cards to our list of current passions for which we needed to make room.

We coughed and sneezed our way through a collection of dusty baskets, some she had been holding onto for years. Susan explained that she liked to make special gift baskets for friends and fill them with goodies for special occasions. I asked her the last time she had given a gift basket, and she couldn't remember. She examined a broken-down old Easter basket she was holding and ruefully commented, "I guess I wouldn't want to receive a gift in one of these nasty old baskets."

We got out the large garbage bags, and Susan pitched the worst of her collection. She got on a roll, and we started a second bag of baskets to be donated. With about ten baskets to go, Susan's enthusiasm slowed, and she began having regrets. She pawed through the Donate bag and reclaimed a few treasures. She pointed at 14 remaining baskets and declared that she needed to keep them. I could practically see the visions of the "pampering spa basket" and the "homemade cookies basket" and the "breakfast basket" dancing through her head as she handled the reedy containers. I smiled inside as we set aside 14 baskets.

A sewing machine and the accompanying notions and fabrics soon appeared. Susan did not have an overabundance of fabric so we easily grouped fabric together into patterns and solids. She had more notions than space in her sewing basket though, so we grabbed some of her 14 baskets and began to sort her small supplies and unfinished projects into those baskets. Each unfinished project we unearthed unsettled Susan, and she seemed itchy to stop our process so she could complete her hobby projects. Because she seemed anxious to pick up where she had left off, I knew that sewing would remain a current hobby that deserved dedicated space in her new hobby room.

At the bottom of several boxes were thousands of loose beads, rolling around like Lucky Charms in a cereal box. I asked Susan if she liked beading as a hobby, and she said that she loved it. We had to dump the beads onto the floor and reunite similar beads into containers. As we sat on the floor sorting, I found hair clips and Campfire Girl vests and craft projects, all adorned with beads. Susan wistfully told me that she used to make special outfits and hair accessories for her daughters with all her beads and thread and notions. As we organized the projects and supplies and laid them in tidy piles, I gently asked Susan if she did any of these projects in her life now. She surprised me by bursting out crying. She admitted that she had not done any beadwork for years. I realized that these materials represented a long-forgotten time for her.

By talking through the contents of each pile, we began to discuss the schools and churches and even recreation centers that might enjoy these fantastic materials for their members. Susan agreed that she would likely not be doing any more beadwork in the future and was comforted by the idea of passing her supplies along to children who could use them. She looked around at her framing and card supplies and said hopefully, "I guess I have enough other hobbies to keep me busy for a while!" I marked *Donate* on a nearby box, we loaded her beading supplies into it, and she looked relieved.

Finally, Susan and I came to the end of sorting her supplies, and our short list of current hobbies included framing, sewing, and card making. Our discovery process revealed that we needed special space for her to work on those three activities.

Next, we measured the room, and I assessed the furniture we had to choose from. Susan had made it clear from the beginning of our work together that she didn't need or want any "fancy, expensive furniture" and that she wanted to make do with what she had. A yellow painted desk with four drawers that had belonged to her daughter became Susan's sewing center. Its drawers offered just enough room to store her fabric and notions. Its surface offered ample space to leave the sewing machine set up for mending on the go. We pushed it against the wall, and Susan enjoyed setting up her new area for sewing.

We had two bookshelves, a few end tables, a folding table, and some stools and chairs left to choose from. We chose the sturdier, nicer bookshelf as our card center. We pushed it against the opposite wall and loaded it to the gills with Susan's cards and card-making supplies. To her delight, I proposed that we use some of her smaller gift baskets as storage containers. We took the baskets that had no handles and the ones that were square and used them to store stamping supplies and ink, embellishments, special pens, and card stock. *Voila!* Susan's card-making center appeared, and she gazed at her baskets of supplies like a kid in a candy store. "Where can I actually make the cards, though?" she asked as she realized that this shelf was for storage only.

I had just set up the folding table to the left of the shelf and showed her how she could spread out here and make cards to her heart's content. Under the table, I set up her frames, starting with the largest at the back, stacking them so she could easily flip through them to get to the size she wanted. I pulled a picnic-sized basket out of her gift basket collection and suggested we keep her smaller frames inside. Susan literally clapped her hands in glee as she picked up on the trend. She grabbed another basket, put it on the floor next to the frame basket and asked, "How about we keep the mat board in here?" I heartily agreed, and before long, we had an organized framing area under the folding table. Its surface would serve the dual purpose of frame assembling and card making.

We set chairs in front of the sewing center and the folding table and stood back to admire our work. We removed the extraneous end tables from the room and broke down the boxes for recycling. We hauled the items to be donated out to her car so Susan could deliver them to charity. For the first time, Susan had a craft room, her very own space to design and create. Energized and overcome, she cried again and hugged me, saying she didn't think it was possible to love a room that much. I still get teary eyed when I think of her, a grandmother, practically hopping up and down with pride in her newfound hobby space.

A Dedicated Room or Multipurpose Space

Not all of us have the luxury of a dedicated room where we can spread out and work on our crafts. The good news is that whether you have a special room or a designated space in a multipurpose room, you can make room for your hobbies.

Obviously, if you have a large enough home or can spare a bedroom, you might want to dedicate a whole room to your pastimes. When you have a special room for your arts and crafts or hobbies, you can go through your supplies as Susan and I did, determine how many stations you might need, and set up the room around your various activity centers. By dedicating the room to your individual pursuits and creating specific stations for each activity, you can streamline your space.

Another benefit of having a dedicated room for your hobbies is that you can choose to invite other hobbyists into your room, and you can work together on your favorite leisure pursuits. Children love arts and crafts rooms and often pick up their parents' hobbies if they are invited to participate and learn.

This might surprise you, but sometimes setting aside a whole room for your crafts isn't a good idea, even if you can afford the space. When we built an addition onto our home for my office, I was finally able to move out of the two bedrooms I had been using for office space. Trevor quickly claimed one of the emptied bedrooms as his hobby room. I was excited for him to have a space where he could work on his model planes, look at his airplane magazines and books, and tinker with his real airplane parts. He had also taken up a new hobby of sewing hunting gear, so we set up his sewing machine and material on a separate table.

He didn't want to spend the time organizing or storing his supplies, so to my chagrin he just spread them all over three tables that were in the room. Soon, the supplies and old magazines and wadded-up fabric erupted onto the floor. That was six months ago, my friends. Even a professional organizer—to her mortification—can temporarily end up with a neglected room! The downfall of Trevor's dedicated hobby room was that he never went in there. It was too far away from where he spends most of his time. He simply added things to the room. He admitted that the room isn't quite what he thought it would be.

If you have a room like this, relocate the hobby or craft items to a place that you actually inhabit regularly. For Trevor, that space would be his garage. Originally, he pulled all his hobbies out of his garage to create his special room, but all he did was shuffle his clutter by resisting setting the room up properly and never making time to go in the room.

Multipurpose rooms, like spare bedrooms, bonus rooms, basements, and garages, may in fact serve your hobby habits and storage needs better than dedicated spaces. If you don't have enough craft or hobby equipment to justify a whole room, you can carve out a space in another room that can become your special space.

I have a client whose three children seemed to take over the whole house and Mom was left with nowhere to unwind and work on her favorite crafts. We solved the problem by building a little workstation into her wide hallway upstairs. It offers her a little getaway and doesn't take up a whole room. Another client set up a scrapbook table in her bedroom because that was the only space she could portion out for herself. She neatly stored her albums and supplies in bins underneath the table and could close the door at night and work on her hobby in relative quiet. Almost any home offers nooks and crannies you can carve out for hobby space.

Actively Using or Simply Storing?

A dedicated hobby room only makes sense if you actually plan to spend time in the room creating and maintaining. Otherwise, your room may quickly become, like Trevor's, a vortex of good intentions! If you don't see yourself climbing the stairs to a distant bedroom or holing away in the basement to work on your hobbies, think twice before setting up a room for this purpose. Look at your natural habits before you dedicate a room to your hobbies. If you more naturally spend time in two or three rooms of the home, ask yourself if you really will break with your habits and retrain yourself to use a dedicated space.

Trevor is not the only one in our home with good intentions. I used to think I would work on my photo albums in my spare room. I set up tables and made all my supplies easily accessible on nearby shelves. But I was lonely sitting up in the room by myself, and the room wasn't really large enough to accommodate fellow scrapbookers. Since I wasn't actively using the room, I found myself gathering my supplies and trekking to the local scrapbook store for the camaraderie (and abundant supply offering) that was available.

An alternative to a dedicated room for hobbies is to assign a series of shelves or a nook in another room to hold your hobby goods until you use them. You can store your equipment and supplies in a spare room as I do, in the hall closet, or even in the garage. Then, when you are ready to create something, you can take out what you need and replace it when you're done. I now store my scrapbook materials in the shelves in the spare room, but I don't expect myself to work on the albums in solitude anymore. I have pared down the quantity of what I own, I only buy supplies when I have a specific need, and I've made my equipment and materials portable so I can easily take them with me. I've allowed myself to store my hobby items in this room without expecting myself to work on those activities there.

In addition to your natural habits, you will want to consider the features of the room to determine if you can frequently and realistically enjoy your favorite hobbies in that space. If you love to paint, for example, and you have a spare bedroom that you could set up as an art studio, think about the features of the space—and the length to which you're willing to go in order to adjust those features. Yes, you may have an extra room you could designate as a studio, but if there is poor natural light, does it really make sense? You might have the room available, but if it is covered in white carpet, you'll have to decide whether you want to replace the flooring, cover the carpet, or skip using that room as your art studio.

Storage and workspace considerations also might help determine whether you should create a separate room or just store your supplies elsewhere. If you work on your hobbies at a certain desk or table, you will want to store the supplies nearby. Many of my clients have children who work on their homework and craft projects at the kitchen table. One of my clients stores her children's arts and crafts supplies in rolling carts in her mudroom, which is adjacent to the kitchen. Another client stores such supplies in the hall closet, and another has cleared out kitchen cabinet space to accommodate these materials. Storing your supplies nearby is a useful and sometimes preferable alternative to having a dedicated room.

Think about your natural habits, space features, and storage and workspace considerations before you preemptively nominate a room for hobby duty. Likewise, you may benefit from some tactical advice and caution when establishing your hobby haven.

Tactics and Traps

Susan and I examined her belongings before we set up a room. In *Reclaim Your Life* I share a key tactic called the Process Principle. I use that principle every day when I'm helping people order their homes and offices. It means that instead of prematurely imposing solutions on a space, you first discover what you want to store and what works for you. You'll note that I followed an investigative process with Susan; I did not presume anything as we began her project. As we progressed, we discovered which activities she had abandoned and which she still enjoyed. We did not decide what furniture and containers we would use until the right time in the process. In other words, we let the project develop around the discoveries we made. This is the Process Principle in action. You can reference chapter 7 in *Reclaim Your Life* if you want to master this principle in your home.

We also chose a specific purpose for her space. We let the supplies and gear develop by quantity. After we had enough of one type of hobby, Susan and I then assigned a purpose to each activity center and made a space for it inside the room. I've found that the only successful way to maintain a hobby room or storage area is to first gather all like items throughout the house. That way, you'll know how many shelves or bins you'll need in a storage area, or whether you can even justify a whole dedicated room. To learn more about how to purpose your space, visit chapter 14 of *Reclaim Your Life*.

My methodology of discovery and purposing has never let me down. If you apply the discovery process and understand how to purpose a space, you can transform any room of your home. Yet you can stumble on certain traps that I've found specifically apply to hobbies and crafts if you are not aware of them. Here are some questions you can ask yourself to avoid hobby room traps:

What Is Important Now?

Remember how Susan cried when she realized that she was never going to rekindle those fond times of beadwork with her daughters? At that point, she made a decision to move on. Many people, sadly, never do move on. They live in the past or in the future. They say to themselves, *I used to love this, so I need to keep it.* Or they reason, *I might find a use for this someday, so I should save it,* or *My kids don't want this, but maybe someday my grandkids will.*

By living in nostalgia or in wishful thinking, people often keep way too much stuff, especially hobby stuff. If you suffer from this problem, determine what is important to you *now.* Resist what used to be important or what might be important and try to stay firmly in the present. You will greatly increase your enjoyment of your home when you can live in the present, and you will have a lot less stuff clogging up your space!

Is It Worth It?

Another easy trap to fall into is buying things just because they're on sale. You know what I'm talking about. Some people just get giddy for a trip to the Dollar Store. Others accumulate way too much overage at the warehouse stores like Costco and other club stores. Many of us just get weak in the knees for a bargain. We pick up little plastic storage containers for practically nothing at the dime store, thinking they will come in handy even though we have no use for them now. We think that if gift baskets are on sale, we should pick up a few for gifts. We don't really know who we are going to give them to, but they are just so cute we can't resist. Items like these often find their way into hobby rooms and stagnate. They collect dust, we trip over them, and we save them for an unidentified date in the future.

If you buy things just because they are on sale, think twice about this reasoning. Consider this: The more extraneous stuff you buy, the less money you have for things that really matter to you. The more items you pack into your room, the less access you have, and your clearly defined activity centers might soon be buried under a pile of gift baskets. Also, your discount deals were bought on impulse, so you didn't think about how you would use them, which makes them hang around even longer until you finally (if ever) discover a use for them.

What Purpose Does It Serve?

Those who have come from a humble financial background might also fall into thinking *It's still good,* or *It still works.* This happens a lot with clothing and household items.

Susan applied the "it's still good" reasoning when she clung to her dusty collection of baskets. You and I would never want to receive a gift in those dirty baskets, but she could not see past the fact that she had gone to all the effort to collect them, and the ones she saved were still—in her estimation—in good shape. Craft supplies, art supplies, and hobby equipment often accumulate because we tell ourselves that the stuff we bought is still okay and that we should use it someday. This reasoning is closely related to the "I paid good money for it" excuse for keeping things. Again, we justify keeping something because we are ignoring our actual need for it, placing a higher priority on how we acquired it and the fact that we own it now.

The only way to overcome these thoughts is to stop the excuses and ask yourself one question: What purpose does this serve? Get practical. Yes, it might still be good or workable, and it might have cost you something. Yet if it is no longer serving a purpose to you, if it is no longer necessary to your life, and if it is not even enjoyable to you, why are you keeping it? If we ask ourselves a similar question—*Do I need this?*—we might be tempted to answer, *Of course!* However, if we force ourselves to ask what purpose something is serving and we cannot come up with a satisfying answer, it may be time to let go!

Refueling Station

A hobby or craft space may seem like a luxury, but we all need a way to refuel our energies, and hobbies can help us to do so. Relaxing into your enjoyable pastimes, working with your hands, and creating something yourself is a wonderful way to restore your mental health.

If you take the time to establish a hobby or craft space in your home that is accessible and customized to your unique endeavors, you will be invigorated with possibilities. If you have tried to set up this kind of location before without luck, I recommend that you start over. Decide whether you need a dedicated location or just a storage area. Apply the tactics I suggest and avoid the traps that can keep you clogged with superfluous stuff. Get ready to refuel!

Part Four

Storage Spaces

Chapter 14: The Closet

Chapter 15: The Garage

Chapter 16: The Basement and the Attic

Chapter 17: The Storage Unit

Public spaces and private spaces inside the home each have their own organizing challenges. Yet the good thing about these spaces is that they are pretty straightforward. It's fairly obvious which items should live in a kitchen or a home office.

Storage spaces, on the other hand, are where we stuff and stash everything else. If an item doesn't seem to go in any of the public or private rooms of our home, we open a closet or cabinet and shove it in. We toss nomadic, unsightly, and cumbersome items into the garage or basement or shuttle them up to the attic. In dire straits, some of us resort to off-site storage if our mess has grown out of control. If you are ready to tame these unruly spaces and finally be able to find something when you need it, part 4 will inspire you to tackle even the scariest storage challenge.

14

The Closet

IMELDA HAD 115 PAIRS OF SHOES. Many of them she could not find because she had kicked them off onto the floor of her closet, and now they were stuck in the dark recesses where she dared not go. The poles supporting her excess of clothing were sagging from the weight, and the hangers were crammed tightly together on the rod. Imelda's closet also held a myriad of items besides clothing, including gift wrap, tissue paper, boxes of all sizes, memorabilia, and handbags.

Her clothes closet was located in the spare room (her husband, Bill, had taken the smaller closet in the master bedroom), so she spread out into the spare bedroom itself. And spread she did. From suitcases to photo albums to jewelry to books to shopping bags full of clothes, Imelda's spare bedroom doubled as her dump-and-go space. Her clothes closet actually became a "closet room."

When Imelda received gifts at Christmas, they landed in the closet room until she could unpack them. The floor was covered with bags filled with the vestiges of shopping trips, and a path led to the door of the closet. Several of the dresser drawers held layers and layers of receipts from all the shopping trips.

Furniture crowded the closet room. Anchoring the room were the guest bed, dressers, and nightstands. When I asked Imelda whether any guests slept on the bed, she admitted that she was the only brave soul that risked the dangers of the closet room to use the bed for an occasional nap. She sent her guests to hotels. On one wall was the computer desk. Stacked on the desk were piles of paper and envelopes of pictures. Imelda was using the closet room as a catchall for everything that didn't have a home, and she had way too much going on in the space.

Neither Imelda nor her husband wanted to rearrange the room or remove any furniture, so my work was cut out for me. My mission was to contain clothes and accessories to the closet and separate the closet from the rest of the room so that Imelda and her husband would once again have a guest room and an office. I needed to organize the whole mess while delineating between the various purposes of the space.

Imelda's exploding closet may sound familiar to you. Many of our clients have catchall rooms. Those dumping grounds often grew from an out-of-control closet. Even if you don't have a whole closet room to organize, you can learn from the closet-organizing strategies I'll share in this chapter. I'll devote most of the chapter to our clothes closets because we all have one (or more) of these, and I'll spend the rest of the chapter briefly covering other kinds of closets.

Clothes Closets

Multiple Closets

Our clothes closets are supposed to contain our wardrobe, shoes, accessories and (we hope) not much more than that. You may have one or more clothes closets. Many people have multiple closets with clothes hanging in them. Imelda's closet inside the closet room contains only the current season of clothes. That's right, twice a year she swaps out her fall and winter clothes for her spring and summer clothes. She has two other closets in the house that contain clothes. That's why a discussion on clothing closets cannot just be limited to the master closet. Your clothes closets are wherever you store your duds.

Personally, I do not swap out my clothes seasonally. I used to do just that, but I found that I was walking back and forth between two closets, searching for all-weather items. I live in Oregon, where the climate lends itself to all-season clothes. Yet I didn't have room for all my clothes in one closet. As a result, I got serious about eliminating the items that I didn't like (you know, the ones that make you feel dowdy or that you bought impulsively but didn't like two days later) or didn't wear. After I had pruned back the excess, I hired a closet company to replace my pole-and-shelf closet system that came with the house. I designed a system that traded long-hang space for short-hang space and included cubbies and a groovy shoe bar for all my shoes. With my new design, all my clothes and Trevor's clothes fit in one closet.

If you have multiple clothes closets, you may not be compelled to get rid of any superfluous clothes or consolidate closets unless you have a good reason. Let me give you a few reasons to consider consolidating. One, searching for things might be causing you trouble and wasting your time (this is what I found). Two, you may be bothered by the fact that certain outfits are neglected, collecting dust, and not being used and enjoyed. Third, you might like to reclaim one of your clothes closets for another purpose.

Clothes Hang-Ups

Many people put off organizing their clothing closets because it can be painful. A clothes closet is an intimate space. In it we store our memories, hang our good intentions, stow our beliefs, and catalog our image.

If you think about it, we often keep clothes because they remind us of special occasions or fond memories. Nothing is wrong with treasuring a bridal gown or special scarf given to you as a gift. When your accumulation adds up to an entire wardrobe from the 1980s, however, you may be facing a problem.

We all have good intentions. Mine have to do with workout wear. I am a charter donor of the YMCA, which is just down the street.

(I figure you only are really a member if you actually attend, so I guess that makes me a donor, writing a check every month but not using the facility.) I intend to get to the gym, but something always seems to get in the way. I've never met a workout outfit, no matter how cute, that made me want to work out. You may have similar good intentions. You might hold onto clothes from bygone sizes or hopeful future sizes. Our good intentions are clogging up our closets and making us feel guilty. Liberating ourselves from these good intentions may actually make room for motivation.

Which clothes we keep offers a window into our beliefs. When I was in high school, I used to inherit all my brother's hand-me-downs. This was great when I inherited polo shirts in 12 colors. However, I also kept flannel shirts and boys' jeans far too long, all with the reasoning, "I can wear these camping." Camping! How often did I go camping? Hardly ever—certainly not enough to merit the space I was hogging with hand-me-downs. Many of my clients have similar reasoning: "What if I need it?" "It's still in good condition." Our faulty thinking is causing us to keep too much deadwood in our clothes closets.

Our closet is also an intimate space where we assemble our image. We walk out of it and face the world. We want to feel good about ourselves. Our clothes, accessories, and shoes say something about us in this appearance-focused society. Our closet is where we keep all our attempts to look right, fit in, and feel good about ourselves.

We sometimes keep too many clothes because they represent memories, good intentions, faulty thinking, and self-image issues. If you go into your closet-organizing project knowing that you will face some of these hang-ups, they will be less startling for you. So get ready to stare down your closet and take back control!

Closet Burn Down
Remove Contents

When I'm organizing a closet, I like to get everything out of the space. Like most other spaces, it must be emptied to experience a true organizing overhaul. You must touch, group, and make a decision about every item before you will be ready to consider your storage system and reload the space. You must deal with each and every item in the total burn down. To learn more about the importance of going to the bottom of the barrel to achieve lasting change, see chapter 12 of *Reclaim Your Life* on the topic of the total burn down. There you'll learn more about Imelda's closet room and how she handled the organizing process.

When I'm gutting a clothes closet, I like to use boxes, bins, laundry baskets, and rolling garment racks. The boxes and baskets capture and sort folded clothes and accessories. Of course, items can be laid on the bed, but you will only have so much surface space for that purpose. A rolling garment rack (which you can purchase, borrow, or rent) will help keep nice hanging clothes wrinkle free during the process. I purchased a few rolling racks for my professional use, and when I'm not using them for clients I use them in my laundry room to stage clothes that need to be steamed or put away.

Micro Sort

When removing contents, I categorize each type of item into a box, a bin, a basket, or a section on the rack. Even the piles on the bed or floor receive labels: Dress Tops, Shoes, and Casual Pants. This way, clients can see all their like items together.

When I began helping Imelda organize her clothes, we grouped all her tops by category. We found that she had 14 black sweaters! Once Imelda could see all her similar sweaters together, she eliminated the old and stained ones and kept only her favorites. Making decisions is easier if you thoroughly sort your belongings.

Too often, we are given bad organizing advice, and we've believed the lie that we should sort into three simple piles: Keep, Toss, and Donate. I cringe when I hear this advice. Think about it—how helpful would a massive mountain of Keep items be if it included mismatched shoes on top of shirts, on top of jeans, on top of socks?

This macro sort really doesn't work, and I recommend the micro sort I've outlined above.

Make Decisions

Organizing a closet is no different from organizing any other space in the home. In order to achieve customized results, I begin by taking time to understand my client's taste and lifestyle. If I am working with a former executive who is now a stay-at-home mom of toddlers, I help her consider whether she would be returning to the work world. If the answer is "years from now" or "never," we know that her lifestyle no longer requires as many suits and professional clothes. If she is a classic dresser and has acquired some flamboyant items on a whim, we can evaluate together whether these items fit her tastes or need to be chalked up to impulse purchases!

When organizing clothes I also take into consideration my client's best colors and size. If we know she looks best in bright jewel tones, why should she hold onto muted earth-tone outfits that she will never wear? If we know she is currently a size eight, why hold onto old larger or smaller clothes? Hanging onto clothes that are wrong for you keeps you stuck in a pattern of what-if thinking.

You can consider your own tastes, current lifestyle, colors, and size to customize your clothes closet. Making decisions about clothes is harder than some other household items, so be gentle with yourself. You can always prune some items now and prune more later when you are ready. On the other hand, a radical pruning now will make more room for your smashing clothes, give you breathing room from too much accumulation, and will allow a little room for growth down the road.

As you are customizing your closet to match your real life, here are some additional questions you can ask to select the keepers:

- Does it fit?
- How often do you wear it?
- Is it out of date?

- Do you love it?
- Does it make you feel fabulous?

Now that you've eliminated your excess, determine whether the items you want to keep can fit into the space. Whenever possible, I recommend that people keep their clothes all together unless space doesn't allow for that luxury. Having a consolidated closet keeps all your clothes in view, so none are forgotten or neglected. It allows you to use and enjoy what you have, which is what organizing is all about!

If limited space doesn't allow you to consolidate all your clothes into one closet, decide which items will live in another location. If you eliminated your shoe shelves in the closet, for example, and made more room for hanging clothes, could you put a shoe bar in an adjacent hall closet? If you moved out all the accessories and handbags and identified a different home for them, could you limit yourself to one clothes closet? If you must separate your clothes, divide them by season (preferably the colder seasons together and warmer seasons together), and be prepared to swap them out semiannually.

Part Well

Clothes can be more sentimental than other items in the home, so my advice is to part with them in a manner that will make you feel good and eliminate separation anxiety. Here are some ideas to minimize your angst:

- Give them to a friend who is your size and can't afford to acquire new clothes or who is returning to work.
- Call your local homeless shelters for men, women, and children to learn their current clothing needs.
- For your maternity clothes, find a charity that passes them along to women with crisis pregnancies.
- For your professional clothes, find a charity like Dress

for Success that outfits needy people returning to the workforce.

- Consign them at a consignment store and use the funds you earn to fill in your new, refreshed wardrobe.

Storage and Style

Now that you've gone through the closet burn down, match your closet contents with the appropriate storage choices. You'll want to consider your visual needs, container choices, and aesthetics in this step.

Are you a "see it" person or a "hide it" person? "See it" people must see it to believe it. If they put something away, it might as well never have existed. Out of sight, out of mind. You will be able to tell if you are a "see it" person if you don't wear anything in your drawers, and you tend to hang things up or stuff them on a shelf where you can track them. "See it" people need clear containers and open shelving to fully enjoy their wardrobe because the minute their items are stored, they disappear from their "radar."

"Hide it" people can't stand the look of clutter. To us "hide its," physical clutter is mental clutter. Nothing bugs us more than sweaters or shirts stuffed in an open shelf. I am mostly a "hide it" person. My husband has cubbies for his work clothes, and I sometimes refold his crumpled clothes so they look nicer in the cubbies and so I can fit more into the space. We put things away and have no fear of losing them because we know exactly where they are: out of sight and thankfully so! We like drawers, cabinets, and doors.

We should choose containers for our closets only after we've sorted through everything and know exactly what we need to contain. Be sure to honor your "see it" or "hide it" needs. Consider ease of access as well as visibility when you are purchasing products. I recommend you avoid stacking bins that have lids on top. If you want something inside the bottom bin, it might seem like too much work to remove the three top bins to get to the bin you want, remove the lid, and fish for your item. I am also not a fan of laundry hampers that have lids for this very reason. If it is difficult to add to or unload, it won't be used as intended. Don't give yourself any reason not to easily access the items you want. If you do want to make use of vertical space, I prefer the plastic bins that have removable drawers instead.

Sweater bags can pose the same problem of difficult access. They seem like a good idea, so you go out and purchase one for each of your sweaters and stack them on the highest shelf. You bought the opaque variety because they were on sale, so you also can't quite see into them. As a result, they collect dust on your top shelf, and you spend many winters with no sweaters, or you buy new ones that you hang up.

More now than ever you can find designer hangers, fabric-lined bins, scarf and tie organizers, and even retro hat boxes. Try to balance style with practicality when it comes to your closet storage containers. You can use baskets, cedar boxes, jewelry organizers, undergarment organizers, and more to personalize your space.

Closet organizing doesn't have to be sterile. Give yourself a full closet makeover. I like using mirrors and color in a closet. After you've gutted the closet of contents, paint the walls and make it bright and cheerful. Upgrade the light fixture if necessary (mine is on a dimmer switch so Trevor doesn't blind me in the morning when he gets up at the crack of dawn.) Design (with the collective help of your organizer and closet designer) and have installed a closet system to maximize your space. Pick a cool, non-white finish like chocolate or mahogany, and soon your closet will feel like built-in furniture for only pennies more.

Of course, if you want your closet to serve pure function, don't worry so much about style and form. It's all about what works for you. Organizing your clothes closet will restore efficiency to your morning and evening routine. The simple fact that you've taken the time for the total burn down will make your closet an easy place to get in and out of without much fuss.

Other Closets

Because closets are storage spaces within the home, the most important thing to remember as you organize them is to step back and understand how this one closet interacts with the rest of the home. Too often, people try to organize a closet by pulling everything out (a good start) and tidying it up (mistake) and shoving it back in (big mistake). This will rearrange the closet, but it won't organize it.

Instead, make sure you know the purpose of each storage closet in your home before you begin your total burn down. Once you know the purpose of the closet in question, gather all related items throughout the house, ensure the closet will accommodate the size and quantity of those items, and only then begin to load the closet.

Children's Closets

You may think your children's clothes closets should be smaller versions of your own process and storage, but they are more prone to season-of-life changes than yours. When your children are very small, they will require more dresser or drawer space than hanging space because most of their clothes can be folded. During this time the closet can be used for toy, equipment, and blanket storage. As your children grow, their clothes will too, and they will likely begin to require hanging space. As this occurs, be prepared to reconfigure kids' closets or dressers or both and change with the times. In children's closets and in the rest of your closets, if you can observe when change has occurred and shift your system accordingly, you will stay on top of household order.

Linen Closet

Another popular closet is the linen closet, where you might store towels, bedding, pillows, and sleeping bags. If you've loaded all your linens into this closet from throughout the house and still have more room, you can consider leaving extra room for more linen acquisitions or expanding the linen closet's purpose to include something else.

If the linen closet is near bathrooms, our organizers will frequently assign a dual purpose for the linen closet to include the storage of overflow paper goods (like toilet paper and facial tissue) or overflow body products (like shampoos and soaps) or even medicines. Storing first aid and medicines in a linen closet will get these items out of damp bathrooms and provide easy access. Be sure to keep them out of reach of little ones to ensure safety.

Household Closet

While they aren't often named the household closet, our organizers see many closets stuffed with extra appliances, china, candles, decor items, and all kinds of household miscellany. I call this the household closet. Sometimes these items are shoved into a hall closet because someone with an armload of stuff saw an open shelf and wanted to unload a pile and shut the door. If you have a closet like this, my first recommendation is to see if you can relocate the miscellaneous items to more appropriate homes: kitchen items into the kitchen, candles into the utility room or wherever you keep them, and so on.

If your household closet feels like a microcosm of the whole house, however, you will not be able to do this easily. Even though this seems like a small space to tackle, all you will be able to do is rearrange unless you have a big-picture plan and purpose for the rest of the home and storage spaces. In that case, wait on organizing this closet until you have determined the purpose and organized more of your rooms and storage spaces. Eventually the contents of the household closet will either be disseminated into sensible, organized spaces, or the closet will become a more mature version of itself, with a shelf intentionally dedicated to each of the household items you want to store.

Activity Closets

Some of us are fortunate enough to have plenty of storage and can designate our closets to store our unique belongings. For the family that likes to play a lot of games and has a closet near the family room or bonus room, a game closet might be a perfect place to store all the puzzles and board games and video games. On a broader scale, some of our clients have an entertainment closet, which includes books, games, music, and videos. Creative people who enjoy making things or folks who have small children to entertain often want a craft room. Since many people don't have an extra room for the purpose of arts and crafts, the next best thing is often a craft closet that stores all their supplies and materials. Scrapbook lovers or those who like to keep their photos organized might dedicate a closet for the purpose of storing memorabilia. A memorabilia closet can contain your photos, trinkets, and memories in one place.

The key to an organized activity closet is to keep the items inside contained in easy-to-remove bins. Portability is the name of the game when it comes to stowing activities. Keeping all your fabric together in a few baskets, stamps in a caddy, and markers in a box will allow you to remove just what you need from the craft closet for an impromptu project. This portability will enable you to do your projects at the kitchen table or on the floor and then return the supplies to their rightful destination.

Supply Closets

I recently organized a gift closet for a client who had accumulated all kinds of gifts to give. Unfortunately, these gifts were stashed throughout the house, so they were collecting dust. We grouped the gifts in bins labeled Adult, Kids, Baby, and Household. That year, she didn't have to buy any Christmas presents! She just went to her gift closet and chose a gift for each person on her list. Organizing your closet storage spaces can help you be a better steward—not only of your current funds, but also of money you've already spent—by making your belongings visible and accessible.

I've also established a party closet for a client who loved to entertain. She had all the supplies and gear for retirement gatherings, fiestas, birthdays of all ages, seasonal parties, and everything in between. We gathered these items from the dark corners of her kitchen cabinets, garage, and attic, and created a party closet with bins for each kind of party. She was thrilled and couldn't wait to throw her next party. We celebrated with a toast. I wouldn't recommend a party closet for everyone because organizing is not a cookie-cutter process. I assess quantity of items before helping clients decide how to designate their closet storage. When one large category begins to emerge, that's when we know that it may merit its very own closet if we have one available.

One client I have appears to live in a satellite office supply store. She does not own a home-based business or have an elaborate home office. She just loves office supplies. During the sorting process, we found reams of paper, mounds of pens, and an array of envelopes, tape, and files, so we determined that she could either part with some of her supplies or create an office supply closet. She voted for the latter, saying that all the supplies were still good and that her kids could use them for school supplies. With her priorities in mind, we set up what looked like a local office supply store right in her hall closet.

As you can see, closets are the storage staple of the household. They are convenient because they are usually scattered throughout the house. They provide quick access to frequently used items. For these same reasons, we often abuse them with our stashing habits. If you want to resolve closet clutter for good, you'll need to take the time to evaluate the household as a whole and determine the purpose of each storage closet. When you go through this process, your disorganization will begin to disappear as your closets serve their own unique, intentional, orderly purposes.

15
The Garage

THE GARAGE IS ONE OF THE MOST TALKED-ABOUT home-organizing challenges. Its messes invoke more family fights than almost any other space. We love to accumulate more and more belongings, and soon our garages are packed from floor to rafter with the stuff we just have to have. We often can't park our cars (usually our second most expensive purchase after our homes) in the garage because there simply isn't room. Our growing, teetering mound of stuff prevents us from using our garage in the ways we want. For some of us, our garage has become a storage unit.

I've seen everything there is to see in garages across America, and I've observed that garage chaos is not determined by region of the country, size of family, or gender of homeowner. Radically disorganized garages are a national epidemic. We store flea market accumulation, neglected and unknown items, and stuff we just can't let go of until our garages bulge. The garage could easily merit its own book, but in this chapter I will attempt to consolidate my key strategies to overhaul your garage.

The Step and Toss

How do our closed-in carports get so cluttered and neglected? The garage is the one place where we toss everything that doesn't have a home. If we don't know where to put it, we toss it in the garage. If we want to get it out of our way or out of our sight, we toss it in the garage. We simply step inside the door (afraid to go much farther into the abyss) and toss whatever is in our hands.

When you find yourself using your garage as a receptacle, examine the root problem. Usually, we toss items in the garage for two reasons. First, we probably haven't resolved all our organizing challenges within the home. If we had, for example, a designated space for overflow pantry items inside, we would not open the garage door and launch cereal boxes or paper towels into this vortex of miscellany. If we had a home for utility items inside in the laundry room, we wouldn't shove lightbulbs and batteries into any space they fit. If you haven't taken the time to designate the purpose of each of your interior storage areas, you will likely turn to the only obvious storage locale in the home: the garage. Second, if the garage captures your castoffs, you've probably never given yourself a total garage overhaul, and this chapter will help you to do just that.

In many garages, our organizers uncover "time capsules"—the frightening results of step-and-toss behavior. A time capsule could be a beach bag with magazines, a work project, and a half-eaten apple from last month. It could be the "company is coming" cardboard box from last summer, filled with unopened mail, school work, and bills. Time capsules suck in important information, and belongings often find their way to the good old garage.

Organize the Garage Last

For the reasons I've mentioned above, tackling a garage is much easier after you have organized the rest of the house. The garage tends to be a dumping ground for all the unknowns throughout the house. Once you determine the purpose of your interior storage and items have destinations within the home, your garage organizing project will be easier.

If you know where everything goes within the home when you organize your garage, many items can be relocated inside. When you come across luggage in your garage and you've previously determined that all luggage will live in your basement, this luggage can be reunited with its counterparts in the basement. When you find boxes of archival paper and memorabilia stuck in the dark corners of your garage and you've already decided that the upstairs hall closet will store all memorabilia, you know just what to do with those boxes you've just uncovered. When the inside of your home makes sense, determining the appropriate contents of your garage will be much easier.

Some people are just itching to dive into their messy garage and begin organizing it, and my advice to wait on the garage project will be disheartening. I'm not saying that you cannot organize your garage first; I'm simply letting you know that it will be much more intuitive and straightforward to organize if you've taken the time to resolve your issues in the house first. Take it from a pro: You're going to have to face your disorganization within the home at some point. Why not do that first and then make your garage makeover your reward?

Planning Steps

Set a Realistic Time Frame

If you want to overhaul your garage, you cannot pick at the problem. You cannot tidy up or shuffle some things around here and there and expect it to all come together. In order for your garage to become and stay organized, you will need to dedicate enough time to work on your project.

We recommend our clients plan a Blitz of back-to-back days— usually two to three whole days—to work on the project. Begin by emptying your garage. In doing so, your belongings will be outside, sitting in your driveway or on the lawn. Obviously, you don't want to leave your things outside, exposed to the elements or to theft for any longer than necessary.

If you live in a remote area where theft won't occur, you can set up a pop-up shade or tarp to keep things dry or cool during the process. If you live in a populated area like most of us, you might want to consider having a portable storage unit (the storage-on-demand industry has boomed in the past few years) delivered to your driveway for this purpose.

Another reason you will want to dedicate a block of time to work on your garage is simple momentum. As you are emptying and sorting and making decisions, you will build up steam. To stop and start your project is to push the pause button and lose momentum. Once you get going, keep going, and you will thank yourself later.

Assemble Your Team

To successfully navigate your garage project, I highly recommend assembling a team of people to help. Your team may consist of two to a handful of people. You have two choices. You can either hire an expert organizer (or team of organizers for that matter) or gather a group of neighbors or friends to work on the project.

The upside of hiring an expert organizer is that you will have an experienced project manager to guide you and your family through a controlled, deductive process. If you select this choice, of course, you will incur some costs, but you will invest in your peace of mind. You will be more likely to get the project done thoroughly and thought-fully with an expert than with friends. Also, you will think fondly of your organizing consultant when you hit the garage door opener every day after your project is complete and you are returning home to a tame, orderly garage. Another benefit of hiring an organizer is that you will not wonder if you asked too much from your friends and neighbors.

The other choice is to gather friends and neighbors to help you overhaul your garage. The popular upside here is that you save money because presumably you won't have to pay these people (unless you have demanding friends). You can make the garage makeover a fun event and include a barbeque or yard sale at the end of the project.

I have a few cautions for you to consider if you select this option. Friends and family may be willing to help, but be sure you have a plan and a project manager (decide if it will be you) to direct the process from start to finish. We've all heard that many hands make light work. However, many hands may also make for much chaos and confusion without a plan and a process. When many people are gathered to help, they will be looking to you for direction. You will be hearing "Where do you want this?" and "Where does this go?" and "Do you want this?" from all sides. And rightfully so. Your helpers will have a lot of questions, and you will need to be prepared to know and explain how the emptying, sorting, and reloading process will go. If you don't know these steps going in, you may become overwhelmed and make snap decisions that you later regret.

Process Steps

Now that you have dedicated adequate time to your garage Blitz and assembled your team, you can begin the organizing process. Be prepared for things to get worse before they get better. Some people become panicked when their mess is disturbed, regardless of how impractical that seems. They couldn't find anything before the organizing process commenced, but the idea that their piles and hiding spots are being dissembled is quite unnerving to them. This fear is only exacerbated by many hands grabbing things and hauling them out into the open. As I discussed in chapter 8 of *Reclaim Your Life,* the process of organization can be an exposing, painful process, and you will need to be prepared for the process to feel a bit out of control.

Empty the Garage and Identify the Contents

After our organizers conduct an assessment process with our clients, they empty the space to be organized. We don't just dive in and drag the contents of the garage outdoors. As we remove each item, we ask clients to identify the type of item it is because we want to understand their language and how they think about things. One person may say that an extension cord is a household item, but another person might say it is an electrical item. As we identify each item, we put it into a unique box or pile that is labeled with the category the client gave us.

We use a lot of boxes when we are organizing a garage. We recommend that our clients go to the local grocery store or liquor store (that always has a surprising array of boxes!) and gather dozens of boxes. Really—you will be shocked by how many boxes you need for this process. Fifty boxes is not too many. Get them in all shapes and sizes. When you have an array of containers to choose from, as you unload and group things, you can sort them into an appropriate box. If you have found a stash of nails and screws, you can sort them into a small box, which will go into a larger utility category. Likewise, if you have found basketballs and soccer balls, you can contain them together in a large box in a recreation category so they don't roll away.

As you begin emptying your garage, your categories begin to emerge. Categories can easily become ensnared because garage items are often gangly and take up a lot of space. Try to keep the categories separate and well labeled. This way your helpers can easily group like things together.

If you don't know what type of item something is, go ahead and create an Unknown category and set those items aside. After all of your other categories have taken shape, go back to this Unknown pile. You will probably be able to distribute some of these items into a known category. If miscellaneous items remain, these may become candidates for departure later.

Determine Categories

After your categories have emerged from the emptying process, you will now need to decide which you should keep in the garage and which should go elsewhere in the home or disappear altogether. Every garage has both essential categories and optional categories. A category that is essential for you might not be essential for your neighbor. Perhaps you do a lot of camping, and therefore an Outdoor category might be required in your garage—but not in his.

These are some common items that I see housed in the garage:

- recycling (newspaper, glass, cardboard, aluminum)
- sports and recreational equipment (balls, bikes, pumps, nets)
- camping and outdoor gear (folding chairs, tents, sleeping bags)
- automotive (chains, oils, filters, car parts, headlights)
- seasonal decor (Christmas, Halloween, Easter)
- overflow pantry items (paper towels, canned goods)
- gardening (lawn mower, yard tools, pots, soil)
- household items (turkey pan, crock pot, fans, old dressers)
- tools and hardware (equipment, hand tools, nails, bolts, saws)

Some of your categories will emerge instantly. You will discover other categories as you go further in the process.

The only way you can determine your categories is to use a discovery process, which involves asking a lot of questions and examining how you spend your time. Do you really fix things and tinker in the garage, or will that happen on the fifth of never? If being a handyman is more a delusion than a deliverable, perhaps you don't really need a Tools and Hardware category. On the other hand, if your garage were finally organized, maybe you would have the room and accessible equipment to tinker to your heart's content. Determining our appropriate categories is a balance between what we want to do and what we will realistically do.

Essential garage categories are in large part determined by that which should not be living here and should be living indoors instead. Does luggage really have to live here, or can it live in the attic or an indoor closet? Does memorabilia need to live in the garage (I strongly urge against it, since paper items are susceptible to heat and damp conditions), or can it live elsewhere in the home?

If you have outbuildings on your property, like garden or storage sheds, this available real estate will reduce the number of categories in your garage. If you can designate a shed for gardening tools, equipment, pots, fertilizers, and soil, for example, you won't need a Gardening category in the garage. When you come across gardening chemicals in your garage, they will be destined for the shed. Your garage project provides the perfect opportunity to consider if you should build or purchase an outbuilding.

If you have other large storage rooms in your home, like a basement or attic, you will also have more options for storage. You can designate your basement for some of your categories, like Outdoor and Camping or Recreation and Sports, and reserve your garage for other categories. An attic might be the perfect place for infrequently used household items and seasonal decor if you are trying to gain space in your garage.

Prune

As you determine which categories you need and want to store in your garage, you will surely come across items that need to go. This is when an outside, objective party can make a big impact on your garage overhaul. Some people simply shuffle the contents of their garage around because they are unwilling to (or unsure of how to) part with anything. I advise making your garage organization project as successful as possible by taking this golden opportunity to separate from some of your unused belongings. Apply the Pruning Principle that I share in chapter 10 of *Reclaim Your Life* to pare down some of your excess.

Sometimes when our organizers are tackling a client's garage, we discover that activities that used to be of interest are no longer timely or important to the client. If clients have hired a yard service, for example, we can let go of gardening equipment and supplies to make room for the things they do need and use. Local charities might be happy to have these castoffs. One neighborhood in our city has a yard-tool sharing service for homeowners who don't want to store a lot of tools. Similarly, clients who never do their own automotive cleaning or mechanical work may not need an Automotive category, and we can help them part with sets of chains they've never used and brand-new cleaning supplies. The homeless shelter I work with has a vehicle restoration program that would be delighted to receive any automotive items like these.

You can likely prune back outgrown children's items. When the children of the household have flown the coop, consider whether you need to store all their baby, toddler, and teenage belongings. If you're under the delusion that you are saving these things for your grandchildren, just think about how long you'll store them, hoping the grandkids will want them. If you are storing these things on behalf of your children, who claim they don't have room for them, decide if you have the space to do so. Without knowing it, you may be acting as a mini-storage unit for your children and extended relatives. If you have the space and are willing to do so, I guess that's fine. However, if you don't have the space and are compromising your own storage needs as a result, I recommend you set a deadline for them to come and pick up their stuff or begin charging rent to demonstrate the value of your space to your family.

Pruning involves ditching the deadwood you have accumulated in your space. Once items have been consolidated by like type into categories, you can purge any excess, broken, or unnecessary items. Going through each category in your driveway to assess its contents takes time, so be sure to allow reasonable time to accomplish this task. It is much easier to ditch the deadwood when you see 14 soccer balls in a Sports category right in front of you than when you find one at a time in a crowded garage. You can quickly eliminate the ruined balls and keep the ones that are still in good condition—that is, if someone in your household still plays soccer!

Finding beneficiaries for your castoffs can make the pruning process easier. Letting your old camping gear go is easier if you know it is going to a homeless shelter. Remember, when you ditch the deadwood, you are making room for the things that are important to you now.

Assign Destination

After you've emptied the garage, identified contents, determined categories, and pruned back unnecessary and superfluous belongings, you are ready to assign a destination to each category. This entails taking a macro view of your garage. You can determine where you want each type of item to live by frequency of use and available space. Recycling, for example, should live near the interior entrance to the home for ease of access. Tools and hardware should live near the workbench if you have one.

In this stage, I recommend you map out your garage with a pen and paper. Create a simple floor plan and decide where you want the primary categories to be placed. Common sense would indicate that gardening items should live near the garage door rather than tucked in a back corner so that you can get to them easily when you are working in the yard.

Think about the concept of "valuable real estate" when considering the space you have available. Parking space and shelves at eye level or within reach are valuable real estate. In other words, you wouldn't want to store the lawn mower in the middle of the garage if your main priority is parking your car inside the garage. Less valuable real estate—very high or low shelves—should be reserved for less frequently accessed items.

Final Steps
Choose a Storage System

Now that you have a simple floor plan and have thought of where each category should live, you can begin to consider the right storage system for you. This is where a lot of people go wrong in their garage overhaul. Somewhere between assembling their team and emptying the garage, they jumped the gun and ran to the warehouse store and bought shelving. If you buy products too early in the process, you are like to acquire the wrong things.

Budget is probably your first consideration. Custom-built cabinets are more expensive than store-bought options. However, customized cabinetry perfectly fits exactly what you want to store. Built-in cabinets, if left behind when you move, can also add value to your home.

I always ask clients whether they want to take their garage storage system with them to the next home. If they do, custom cabinets can generally be taken off the wall and transported to the new home as long as the cabinets are not overly tall or odd-shaped to accommodate a specific garage, in which case it would be better to leave them behind. Purchasing a modular system like open racks that can be moved around is also a great option for those who want their storage system to be transferable between households.

I also like to take into consideration clients' visual needs. If they want a spotless garage, they might appreciate built-in cabinets, which give a streamlined appearance. Built-ins also offer cabinet doors that can hide your clutter. On the flip side, some people forget what they have if it is stored behind cabinet doors, and for them, open shelving would be preferable.

Many people mistakenly believe that if they just have storage shelves, their organizing problems will be solved. If clients rush out and purchase shelves and racks but have no overall plan for the space or knowledge of the size and quantity of items they want to store, their satisfaction with their purchase will plummet, and they will become frustrated. If you truly want to become organized, you will invest the time up front to examine the items in your garage and categorize them effectively to inform your storage decisions.

Reload

Good news! After you've reached this stage of the process, you are nearing the finish line! Now that you've assessed the quantity and size of items in each category and acquired appropriate storage, all you have to do is set up your storage system according to your floor plan and reload.

This is the right time to replace those grocery-store boxes you used to sort your belongings with permanent containers. Obtaining new storage containers is not a priority for some people, and they will simply put mismatched cardboard boxes onto the shelves and into the cabinets. If you choose to do this, just remember to keep them well labeled. Be sure to store items that need to remain weather safe in covered bins. Covered plastic bins are sturdy and pest resistant, and some are also water resistant. Clear bins have the added advantage of displaying your items so you can see the contents at a glance.

Maintain

Maintaining your garage order begins with following the process I've described above. If you've cut corners and simply shuffled your belongings, I cannot guarantee that your state of order will last. If you've invested in going the distance and you've engaged in the necessary discovery process, I can promise you that with a little maintenance, your garage will continue to feel like a whole new world.

I recommend that you commit to using my Only policy from chapter 14 of *Reclaim Your Life*. Now that you've limited the categories of items you store in your garage, be sure to discipline yourself to *only* storing those kinds of supplies in the garage. By keeping your categories intact and only adding like items with each category, you will prevent dumping and stashing.

Lastly, commit to a regular schedule of maintenance for your newly organized garage. Set a semiannual date with yourself for a garage tune-up, and you will protect the order you worked so hard to achieve. Between tune-ups, promptly putting things away after each use will also help you maintain order. Even though a garage overhaul is one of the most ambitious projects you can take on, it is one of the most rewarding. If you are ready to invest in the process I've shared, you will join the hundreds of clients who have restored order to their garage for good!

16

The Basement and the Attic

WE JUST LOVE TO STASH STUFF in the outermost reaches of our home, don't we? Many of us who have a basement or an attic can testify to the black-hole effect of these storage spaces. Since they are usually large, expansive areas that are out of our daily sight, everything that is in limbo tends to gravitate to these storage vortexes. Basements and attics have unique advantages and features, but they both tend to become household wastelands. If no one takes the time to assign specific purposes to the basement and the attic and determine what kind of items should live in each space, everyone in the household is likely to abuse this abundant real estate.

The Basement

Jayna has a concrete basement with tiny windows to the outside world. Her home was built in the 1920s. The stairs descend into the middle of the basement, so the space is divided into two halves. On one half is her home office, and the other half houses the family's laundry room.

Because the space is dark and has cold floors and walls, Jayna doesn't get down to her home office very often. It feels like a cave to her, and she is isolated from the rest of the family when she is working. Yet the basement offers the only space in the household where Jayna can set up a home office; all other rooms have been spoken for. Often, moms like Jayna have to take the least desirable room, farthest away from household life, to set up a space for themselves.

Mountains of dirty laundry are scattered all over the laundry room floor. That's because everyone opens the door to the basement and hurls dirty laundry down the stairs, hoping the clothes will land in the general vicinity of the laundry room. But that's not all that inhabits the laundry room floor! The family's bikes are parked in the laundry room because it has an exterior door. Because this space provides ingress and egress, the bikes, trikes, lawn shoes, and coats are strewn about inside the laundry room, chronicling the family's in-and-out activities.

In addition to outdoor gear, the basement has also accumulated items that Jayna intends to give to someone else, purchases she intends to return, and gifts to be given. It is also the final resting place of outgrown toys and clothes that Jayna can't part with. The fancy china, snow clothes, patio furniture, and everything in between also inhabit the basement because these items have no place to live within the home. As a result, Jayna's office and the family laundry room have morphed into one supersized junk room.

Stashing Central

The basement has many of the same attractions as the garage; regardless of how you intended to use it, your good intentions are overwhelmed by step-and-toss behavior (see chapter 15). The basement's vast, open space beckons castoffs of all descriptions. It usually has easy stair access, which invites family members to deposit items on the stairs or stash them out of sight in the dark recesses of the basement.

Even if basements are being used for home offices or laundry rooms, they still attract items that need to be stored! At least with garages, we know that we are supposed to park our car in there and store certain categories of things. Yet we're not quite sure how we should use the basement. We tend to treat it as a catchall space.

Factors Determining Use

Necessity

The most basic factor that determines how best to use your basement is pure necessity: If you've run out of space in the rest of your home for crucial activities or storage, you must look to the basement as potential real estate. Like Jayna, you might need a home office but have nowhere else in the home to turn. These days, having a command center of your household is a necessity. We all need a place to pay bills, manage household projects, juggle family schedules, use the computer, and file our records.

If you have an unused or ill-used basement, my advice is to figure out what kind of space you need but don't have (such as a home office, playroom, or art studio) and look to the basement to see if it can fill that role. Of course, you may have to clear out your basement in order to make way for its new purpose. Even though this will take an investment of your time and will likely require you to eliminate some superfluous stuff, converting your basement to a purposeful use will be far better stewardship than moving or remodeling.

Condition

Another factor to consider as you evaluate your basement's potential is its condition. If you have an unfinished basement with a dirt or concrete floor and stud walls, you probably don't want to establish a playroom there! If you have a sump pump in the basement that must pump around the clock to keep the water table under control, you shouldn't consider the basement as a viable home office space. Likewise, if you get frequent leaks or have a mold problem or some other issue, delay converting the basement to active use until you can resolve these issues.

Most basements can be remodeled and upgraded to take care of all of these problems. Yet you may not be able to put in the kind of money a remodel requires. By the time some people are done with a costly remodel, they could have purchased a larger, more accommodating home! If you can't afford to remodel the basement but need the storage space, you can at least identify items that can live in the basement and endure its current condition. For example, if the floor is dirt, you can store your bikes in there without any problem. You can also store plastic bins with lids to contain your camping and outdoor gear.

Beware if your basement's condition includes water and mold issues. These typically are crucial problems to fix even if you can't justify the cost of a remodel. Water destroys and mold spreads, and both of those issues will likely get your homeowners' insurance cancelled, render your home a health hazard, and make it impossible to sell.

Enduring a disruptive remodel to improve the basement's condition may not be worthwhile if you will be moving in the near future unless you're sure it will radically improve the value of your home. Lastly, you don't need to improve the condition of the space if it is perfectly serviceable now. If you can live with concrete floors and stud walls while you're conducting business in your home office or doing laundry, then you can get on with making your basement a useful extension of interior living space.

Exterior Access

Jayna's bikes and her incoming and outgoing items land in her basement because her basement features a door to the outside world. Whenever I see a door inside a basement, I carefully discuss it with the client. Sometimes people tell me they never use the door, and it's almost as if it didn't exist. They know their home best, but I encourage them to get a heavier door and a dead bolt because I've known too many clients and friends who have experienced intruder invasions through a basement door or window.

The door provides a significant organizational clue because it indicates a likely flow of traffic, and we can usually discern what kind of traffic that is by observing the remnants! Often, organizing is like following the trail of Hansel and Gretel and picking up the bread crumbs left behind. If I find bags of aluminum cans and newspapers and plastics stacked in front of the door, no one needs to tell me that the adults use this access to put out their recycling. If I discover child-sized rainboots covered in mud and trikes and bikes on the basement floor in front of the door, I know that little ones experience playtime just outside this entrance. I share more about my deductive organizing discovery process in chapter 7 of *Reclaim Your Life*. Visit this chapter if you want to learn more about how to assess a space using my discovery process.

If I discover a door that is frequently used, I will often suggest to a client that we set up a mudroom. By carving out a mudroom just inside the door, we can purposefully set up the space around its actual use, whether it's for recycling, stowing coats and shoes, or loading and unloading the family car. Jayna needs a mudroom in her basement because currently all her "clues" are covering the floor and taking up space in her laundry room. By creating a space designed to ease ingress and egress just inside your basement door, you can provide you and your family an orderly transition in and out of the home and limit creeping clutter!

Access to outside from a basement can help you determine how you want to use this space. Perhaps you want to build your basement's purposes precisely around what the door suggests: activity and traffic! If that is the case, you might think about using your basement to serve all your outdoor activities and store their equipment: camping, hiking, boating, and running. Your canoe, portable grill, and running shoes can live in the basement. If your door opens to a patio or backyard, you also might consider using your basement to store gardening tools and equipment. Clearing the Outdoor and Recreation and Yard categories from your garage may actually make more room for cars!

Flooring

As I alluded to in the section on your basement's condition, the flooring of your basement can determine what items you can store in this space. A mud floor might not be a problem if it is servicing the yard and garden, but it would not be appropriate for an office.

Fortunately, some inexpensive solutions for poor flooring are available. You can simply lay down plywood, cardboard, or a weighted tarp if you need to use your basement to store plastic bins. These fixes are not upgrades, but they will maximize your available real estate for storage.

The alternative, of course, is to remodel and upgrade the flooring to accommodate the purposes you want rather than the purposes you're stuck with. Keep in mind that sometimes we can go to great lengths to find a cheap and easy work-around that wasn't in fact the best solution. Working with a professional organizer who is savvy in space design will help you determine the highest and best use of your basement.

Lighting and Heating

Basements that are short on finishing touches can present challenges. Inadequate lighting and heat control can run even the most dedicated office worker or laundress out of the basement. If you intend to use your basement daily or weekly as interior space, you will likely need to invest not only in appropriate flooring but also lighting, heating, and cooling. Making your basement livable for its inhabitants is the first step to organizing. Once you address those factors, you can determine the basement's purpose or multiple purposes and design the space around your desired use.

Basement Buildup

Too often, we use our large, undefined storage space as a dumping ground for nomadic items. Our basements become recesses of confusion and clutter. Instead of making a decision about something, we can toss it in the basement because we reason to ourselves that we have the space. Yet all our reasons falter when we survey a basement layered under years of accumulation, delayed decisions, and miscellany.

Rid yourself of the household black hole. If you've become a victim of basement buildup, now is the time to pay the piper and roll up your sleeves. In order to dig out, you will have to empty the space, evaluate the factors I've described above, and redesign the space. This will take time and (I recommend) a team of people. Basements can hold a lot of stuff, so emptying them is quite an undertaking. The reward, however, is a reclaimed space that will finally serve your needs.

The Attic

My parents have an attic over their garage. I spent countless hours in the attic when I was growing up. To me, it was such an inviting, clever, secret place. Sure, you had to climb up a ladder and mount the edge to get inside, you had to stoop to move around, and its wooden beamed floors didn't seem all that sturdy to me, but I loved it anyway. My taller brother didn't seem that enamored with the attic, which made its privacy all the more appealing to me. I could imagine my very own house among the luggage and boxes and Christmas decorations and old furniture. My attic world ignited my imagination, and from it I commanded ships, hid from bad guys, and dreamed up story lines.

As attics generally do, ours attracted all kinds of items that were stuck in decision-making purgatory. I wondered why my mom's vintage skis were stashed in the corner and why we were keeping the old, torn cover to the pool. Once suitcases came out that had wheels and telescoping handles, I didn't know when we would actually use the leather, non-wheeled, lugging kind that we had. At least a half dozen old suitcases sat abandoned in the attic.

Some useful things lived in the attic, like our holiday decorations and boxes. As every holiday rolled around, someone (usually me because I was small and eager) dashed up the ladder into the attic to hand down the desired items. My mom or dad stood on the ladder and peered over the edge of the attic to direct me to the proper box. I would uncover the box, drag it to the edge, and hand it down, stooping all the while. Boxes that might come in handy populated the attic in ever-growing numbers. My parents prided themselves in always having just the right size box for shipping something. When we needed a box, I scurried up the ladder and, like a store clerk, offered up their choices from the ledge of the attic.

Not-So-Easy Storage

Access

If your attic has some of the same challenges as mine, your childlike attic wonder probably wore off a long time ago. You often have to climb up a ladder or through a low door to get inside these out-of-the-way spaces. This makes access difficult, and retrieval of goods is often a two-person job.

Several of my clients have fold-down ladders into their attics, and other clients have the traditional extension ladder we had. Some have attic spaces that are accessible through dormer or bedroom doors or up a remote staircase. Difficult access into an attic decreases its frequency of use. This causes backlog to pile up in other places.

If your attic space is challenging to access, I advise that you use this clue as a strong caution against storing items in the attic that you need more than once or twice a year. This makes the attic an appropriate storage destination for holiday and seasonal items that you will get out and keep out for a while (like summer gear, such as fans, portable air conditioners, and electric bug zappers). If you stuff items in the attic like your box collection, as did my parents, you will be in and out of this frustrating space more than you want to be.

Safety

Once I reached the top of our ladder, I had to pull myself up into the attic, leaving one foot on the ladder and stretching the other leg onto the floor of the attic. In one shaky, tentative move, I had to leave the safety of the ladder and slide across the splintered floor into a pile of boxes. I eventually became good at this move, but I always pictured myself in a puddle on the floor at the bottom of the ladder.

The pitch of the attic ceiling was steep. Large roofing nails stuck out of the plywood between the beams. More than once I caught my scalp or something I was carrying on these rusty old nails. I could see through the slits in the creaky floor and talk to anyone below who happened to be in the garage. Even though I never fell, I pictured my dad's crushed vintage car if I were to tumble through one day.

Attic safety concerns deserve your attention. Attics are usually unfinished, so they can pose real dangers to the unaware or too-young visitor. If your attic has safety threats, I advise resolving them before you use it as an active storage space. If you choose not to resolve them, proceed with caution when deciding what to store here. Avoid keeping items in the attic that must be stored in moisture- and temperature-controlled environments (such as paper memorabilia, photos, and candles).

Mobility

If you must stoop to move around in a space, you probably won't use it very often. Bear mobility in mind when you begin storing items in your attic. In small spaces that are difficult to navigate, many jobs call for two people. For this reason, seniors and people who live alone will rarely access their attic items. They may not mention limited mobility as a reason they haven't retrieved the fan when it is 80 degrees in their house, but they do avoid the space.

Hectic Holidays

Certainly, attics can provide useful storage for our infrequently used goods. They are ideal storerooms for seasonal items. Yet attics aren't always that easy to use even when you limit yourself to these types of items.

My client Samantha stored her holiday decorations in her attic, which seems to make sense since they are only pulled out once a year. The problem was that her life moves so fast, she is invariably scrambling up and down the ladder at the last moment every year to retrieve the St. Patrick's box. She then hurriedly sprinkled her shamrock decor across the house. The St. Patrick's stuff sat out until Easter because it seemed like too much of a hassle to put the green things away in the distant attic above the garage. At Easter, the scenario repeated itself; she was going at mach speed and never getting things out and back in time. I was once at her house in March and still found Christmas stuff displayed because she hadn't had the time and energy to put it away. This is a common phenomenon in cluttered homes. Often, people stash holiday decorations into the bathroom cabinet or the hall closet because they don't have the energy to put them away in their attic destination.

Samantha's basement had better accessibility than her attic. We relocated all her holiday and seasonal decorations from her cramped attic to her basement shelves. First, we gathered all her holiday items from every place they had been concealed and stashed throughout her entire home. She was amazed when even the coat closet and kitchen produced hidden holiday items! We then organized her decor by each holiday or season into its own bin. Christmas decor required a whole series of bins. We used clear bins and placed their labels prominently. Since her basement was a quick run down a flight of stairs and the shelves were easy to reach, she could set up and put away her decorations far more easily. Samantha also found that with improved accessibility, see-through containers, and clear labels, she could recruit her children to help put things away.

Orderly Storage

Organizing your basement and attic begins with an understanding of the limitations of each space. If you take heed of these obstacles and let the spaces reveal what should live inside them, you will be much more likely to store the right stuff inside and use them more often.

In the process of clearing out and clarifying the purpose of your large storage spaces, you will likely be able to prune back a lot of your excess. Getting a dumpster, or at least some big garbage bags, and sending your castoffs to charity or to the garbage bin will make you feel great. After the pruning has taken place, reload your space with the items you now know will make sense for the space. If you hardly ever use your basement and attic but insist on keeping your treasures in them, you might even consider making a brief list of what you have stored in these spaces so that you know what is up or down there two years from now when you want to find something.

My final advice to you on these expansive storage areas is this: Set aside enough time for your project. When I organize these spaces with a client, I block out back-to-back days (usually a two- or three-day Blitz) to accomplish the project. This way you will have adequate time to consider the types of things that are currently living there, the limitations of each area, and how you will reconfigure the use of the space.

When you Blitz a large storage area, the results benefit the whole family. You will become aware of what you have and make it accessible. You will eliminate things you don't need, and you'll feel good about letting them go. You will locate items in destinations that make sense. Once an item has been used and it's time to put it away, everyone will know its destination and will be empowered to put it away themselves. Orderly storage spaces invite family participation and yield better household management.

17

The Storage Unit

DIANA CALLED ME FROM TEXAS. She had seen me organizing on television and wanted one of my consultants to help her get organized. She needed help clearing out her storage unit, which was packed with forgotten household goods. Diana and her husband had moved six years prior. The move between households had been hectic, and they never settled into their 3700-square-foot home properly. Her proof of the bad move was that many of their household belongings were still in storage six years later!

Diana couldn't remember exactly what was in the storage unit; it was all becoming a fuzzy memory to her. I asked her how often the family went to the storage unit, and she replied that they went there only when they needed something. The whole family was annoyed that they didn't have things on hand that they needed throughout the year, like holiday decorations. Every festive occasion, Diana had to drive over to the storage unit, dig through a sea of boxes to snag a few that were within reach, return home, and put up at least a show of holiday spirit. Months later, she would drive back and redeposit the boxes of holiday items to get them out of her way.

The Cost of the Status Quo

Diana was frustrated because she had to purchase items that she was confident they already owned but had lost in that storage unit. She knew, for example, that they owned camping gear, but it was buried under too many other items to retrieve. When Diana's husband got the itch to camp last summer, they had to buy a new tent, sleeping bags for everyone in the family, and a camp stove. You would think that the needless cost of these duplicate items would have been an incentive to buckle down and get organized. However, Diana and her husband just continued with the nonsensical status quo to avoid the hassle of clearing out and eliminating their storage unit. Still, its existence was plaguing Diana with guilt that cropped up every now and again. I think that guilt was the real reason for her call to me.

When I explained how our services worked and that we would need to fly a consultant to her area for a few days to help her dig out, Diana began to get price conscious. When she learned of the investment she would need to make to empty the storage unit, haul the contents back to her home, and restore order to her household, she said that she just didn't think she could afford it. I asked her how much her storage unit cost each month, and I was astounded—$375 per month! Quickly, I did the math and gingerly informed Diana that she was spending $4500 per year on her storage unit. She sounded surprised, which shocked me all the more. She had apparently never multiplied $375 by 12!

These unnecessary funds were going to house stuff that she had mostly forgotten about, barely used, and was duplicating with new purchases. Even if she didn't hire us, I urgently wanted to help Diana see that she just *had* to do something about this enormous waste of money. We could refer her to an organizer in our network in her area, at the very least, but this woman and her family needed to rid themselves of this storage unit!

Diana then pulled out a classic excuse: "I don't know how my husband would feel about spending the money. I'm going to have to talk to him about this." I fully respect spousal support in all major family financial decisions, so I quietly asked Diana, "Is he aware that you guys have spent $27,000 in the past six years on storing this stuff?" Diana didn't really have an answer for me, and I could tell that this was a not-so-little secret that she kept hidden so he wouldn't freak out.

I asked Diana what she would rather be doing with the $375 per month, and she said she would love to give it to their church. She recognized that flushing this much money down the drain every month was very poor stewardship, but she was clearly counting the cost of the time, energy, and money needed to stop the bleeding of waste. Sadly, Diana ended the call by telling me how much she loved what we do and that she was sure they needed us but that she would call me if she became ready for this process. Diana was being penny-wise and pound-foolish.

For $27,000, you can send a kid to college these days. That will even pay for one year at an Ivy League school! Or you could buy a brand-new sport utility vehicle or make a down payment on a house. Diana had slowly siphoned $27,000 from her family's funds over the course of six years to keep her stuff somewhere else. Seems kind of crazy, doesn't it?

Cashing In on Our Overage

MSN reports that one in eleven Americans now owns a mini-storage unit, so a lot of people like Diana are paying big bucks to keep a roof over their castoffs.[1] This statistic is up 75 percent in the last eleven years and 24 percent in the last two years. This means we are accelerating our desire to collect and keep more stuff and are rapidly claiming mini-storage real estate for ourselves.

If one in eleven households doesn't sound like that much to you, consider this: The MSN report went on to say that more than 40,000 facilities across the country dedicate 1.875 billion square feet to storage units. The storage industry's revenues now exceed that of Hollywood. Several storage companies have made such amazing profits in recent years that they have gone from privately

---

1. Tom Vanderbilt, "Self-Storage Nation," www.slate.com/id/21228321

held entities to public companies. Everyone is recognizing that the personal storage industry is ablaze with growth, and the savvy are cashing in.

I did a quick search on storage unit prices in my area, and I found the Public Storage website, where the home page promised me that "Your stuff will be happy here." Disenchanted, I visited the Shurgard website—one of the public, thriving storage companies—and I found that I could price and even add a storage unit to my online shopping cart! I could retain a five-foot-square, unheated, unlighted spot of this apparently hot real estate for about $50 a month, plus a $22 administrative fee. If I wanted a 12-foot by 30-foot space to store a lot of stuff, I would be looking at $260 per month, plus the administrative fee. At least according to this company, people in my area are paying between $600 and $3120 per year to keep their stationery bikes and toddler hand-me-downs in padlocked safety.

But most people don't spend only 12 short months in a unit; the MSN article also mentioned that the average stint in one of these facilities is 15 months! You can do the math just like me; nothing is "mini" about the price tag of longevity in a mini-storage locker. Storage units, extensions of our overstuffed households, are costing us thousands of dollars that we could be using for more fruitful purposes. They are draining our resources and heaping guilt on our heads. Because it's so easy to leave it and forget it, we do just that. After all, our stuff is happy there!

By the way, finding these statistics online is not easy. Storage unit associations publish magazines and journals online, but those are for subscribers only. Do you really think that the investors and owners of these companies want you to do the math? Do you think they want to make it easy for you to count the practical cost of your storage decision? No! They want to make it easy for you to store and walk away, preferably for a very long time.

Social Disorganization

Because the storage unit has become a popular, albeit often secret, extension of our homes, I think it is important to talk about them in a book about organizing your home. If you really want to get to the bottom of your disorganization and find a long-term resolution, you've got to be willing to consider all your belongings in the process, including the ones you store off-site. Mini-storage units aren't the only destinations for our household goods; many people store their stuff in other people's basements or in outbuildings on their own property. To pull out the entire root of the weed of disorganization, you must consider all your stuff as you are pruning back your overage.

We all have overage—the superfluous accumulation that is burying us alive. It's filling up our crowded homes. To accommodate our growing belongings, our home sizes have increased in recent years. According to the National Association of Homebuilders, the average home size grew from 1660 square fee to 2400 square feet in 2004. Our homes have gained on average 740 square feet, and yet that's still not enough. Our consumer habits are outpacing our space, so we now require almost two billion square feet of storage in addition to our sprawling homes!

Let's face it; getting new things is nice. I like going to Target occasionally to buy something new and trendy even though I know it will shrink or break pretty quickly. But shopping and accumulating can become so habitual that we actually begin to compromise our quality of life. Many of our clients are in this position. I call this way of life "social disorganization." Often unknowingly, we are responding to social and familial norms to accumulate stuff. To learn more about social disorganization and discover whether this might be one of the causes of your disorganization, visit chapter 3 of *Reclaim Your Life.*

Why We're Storing

We can all see that adding to our possessions is, in part, what causes the need for storage units. But sometimes we aren't accumulating new stuff; we just can't let go of the old stuff. We don't want to let go of gifts, hand-me-downs, or sentimental belongings. For a host of reasons, we feel as if we can't part with our stuff. Yet we can't live with it crowding our space, so we push it to the outer limits of our consciousness—our very own off-site storage unit.

Have you ever told yourself that some of your stuff is just too good to get rid of? Have you thought twice before parting with something, reasoning, *I paid good money for that?* Or do you promise yourself that you will sell the item at a garage sale or even at an online auction because it's too nice to donate? Many people who declare they will sell something don't have the time to hold a garage sale or the computer skills to list it online. Our self-deceiving thinking keeps our stuff in limbo. Some of our clients have a closet or even a spare room dedicated to stuff they can't let go of.

If you own or invest in a storage unit company, you may be thinking I have something against the industry. In fact, I do not. I believe there is a time and a place for using temporary storage. Those times include, among others, moving, a life transition like a remodel or divorce, or to store critical business documents (as a business expense). Our organizers recommend a local storage company and on-demand storage unit deliveries in certain circumstances. However, we never recommend that people commit their monies over a long period of time to storing stuff they just don't want to take the time to deal with; this is simply poor stewardship of resources. Short-term use of storage units may make sense in the right circumstance. In my opinion, long-term use of self-storage rarely makes practical or financial sense.

Facing the Music

I had been working with Teresa for two years before she confessed to me that she had a storage unit—well, actually two storage units.

She was ashamed to admit that she had more undisclosed belongings. One day as we sat at her kitchen table, she phrased it like this: "Well, Vicki, I have a dirty little secret I've been meaning to tell you." Her husband didn't even know about one of them. Every month as she paid the bill, she chided herself for not dealing with the problem. For some reason, writing a check became easier for Teresa than facing her storage units.

Upon learning about Teresa's secret, I encouraged her to let me help her eliminate the guilt and deal with her space. Since we were nearing the end of her home organization, I smiled and said, "At least now we will have space to put some of the things we find!" She laughed in relief and we set a date to unlock the unit and face the music.

As part of your home organization project, I recommend you tackle your storage unit last. This way, the rest of your home will have clearly designated storage areas, and you will have an accurate understanding of where each type of item should live within your home. Also, if you wait until the rest of your household makes sense, you will more accurately be able to assess the remaining space you have available.

Do the Math

Friends, I'm going to be brutally honest to help you face the music because I want to drive home a point. You know that I support you in your home organization project. I want to walk through it with you every step of the way. Yet sometimes we have to stare down the pain and get through it if we want to come out on the other side. Facing the storage unit might be painful for you. Until this chapter, it was a little-discussed orphan that you could disregard when you thought about organizing your home. And now, uncomfortably, I've brought it to light. Just know that I'm giving this advice because I care, and I want you to truly go the distance in your organizing journey. I want you to achieve lasting change, and I especially want you to reduce the waste you've been experiencing. When it's all over, I want to hear your stories about how you've found another, better use for those monies. I want freedom for you.

If you haven't confessed your secret to anyone or are delaying doing something about your storage unit, I recommend that you add up the cost of your investment. You could have taken that money and put it toward other uses, like college or braces or a family vacation. Instead, you chose to store stuff. Take the monthly price and multiply it by how long you've had it.

How much have you invested in your storage unit? What have you gained from your investment? Has it been worth it? Now, tell someone your total investment. Getting it out there will make you more resolved to seeing this problem to the end and you'll begin to rue every month that passes without resolution. Ask your confidant to help keep you moving and accountable.

Pay the Piper

In *Reclaim Your Life,* chapter 12, I share a concept called "paying the piper." Instead of belaboring the effort and recounting the reasons we cannot do something, we must pay the piper, step up to the plate, and deal. Many of us, like Diana, will continue to count the cost of dealing with the storage unit. It is out of our immediate domain, so we will find lots of reasons we can't empty it.

Out of sight, out of mind, right? Not really. Most of us have enough financial sense to feel some guilt about the storage unit after a reasonable time has passed. I promise you, the cost and guilt will only continue to grow over time. If you have a lingering storage unit sapping your money, now is the time to dig in, pay the piper, and rid yourself of this drain.

Address Faulty Thinking

As you are standing in the storage unit pitching boxes into a truck bed and tossing out garbage and unnecessary items, look around and ask yourself if all this stuff was worth the hundreds or thousands of dollars you've paid to store it. Since you're paying the piper, you might as well go all the way and learn from this. Ask yourself why you haven't done this sooner, and why you've kept all these things to begin with. Consider what reasoning you used to retain this space for so long, and if it was faulty reasoning, commit to never getting back in this position again.

Pain can be a powerful teacher. Even though it might be easier to skulk through the gate and sneak your stuff out, taking your guilt with you, I encourage you to face down the reasons you ended up here and learn from them. Through your bravery, you will better be able to let go of the guilt, move on, and prevent wasteful decisions like this in the future.

Assimilate

Whether you sort and toss at the storage unit or back home, I strongly recommend that you spend some time to go through your belongings and make decisions. Resist the urge to relocate the contents into your garage, creating a new problem. Get up early on a weekend, gather some friends, and transport your belongings home. Then spend the day or two grouping items by like type, assessing them, and making decisions about their destination. By now, a lot can probably go to charity. Assign someone to itemize your belongings and load them into another vehicle. At least by taking a tax deduction you will be able to recoup some of your investment. You will need to assimilate the items that remain into the proper places in your home if you have the room.

Throw Away the Key

Before you feel as if you are the only one living with a storage unit secret, I want you to know that you are not alone. One of my clients has a storage unit dedicated to the sole purpose of storing her Christmas decorations. Another client hasn't tackled her storage unit because she lost the key to the padlock. Storage units are like bad relationships; we all have our reasons why we have them and why we can't get rid of them.

212 ■ Restoring Order to Your Home

You may have a very good reason for why you need a storage unit, and I've listed some of those reasons above. You may have another reason that I haven't mentioned, like using it for office space. Maybe you can afford to have year-round offsite storage, and yours has never plagued you with guilt. In these cases, you can write off this chapter and apply the rest of what you've learned throughout this book.

Yet, if you're like Diana, I bet deep down you know that a continual substantial investment in potentially unnecessary storage is actually robbing you of funds that you could apply to other purposes. If Diana continues with her storage unit for another few years, she could have afforded to build an addition onto her home! If you have superfluous stuff in a storage unit that is draining your emotions and pocketbook, I invite you to take the first step to throwing away that padlock. Make the commitment to ditch the storage unit by setting a date on your calendar, arranging a truck, and gathering friends or a professional organizer to help. Prepare to free up your funds and your peace of mind!

Make Room for Living

CONGRATULATIONS! TOGETHER WE HAVE WORKED through every room of your home, from public to private to storage spaces. I hope by now you have become a detective, engaging in the discovery process we've discussed. In so doing, you've gained more self-awareness and identified the factors that have contributed to your disorganization in the first place. You've picked up new methodologies, from executing the physical process of organizing to choosing the work style that best suits you. Because you've put in the sweat equity and gone the distance, you have begun to see tangible change in your space. Best of all, your mind has begun to clear as your home has come into more orderly focus.

You know by now that we cannot impose a solution on your space and expect it to last. The only organizing solutions that will endure are those that you discover. If you are not the only one living in the home, you have begun to consider the people you live with and their interests and preferences, and you are empowered to create systems that make sense to all users. Using the clues you discover about each room and the family's habits, needs, and tastes, you are better equipped to establish systems that really work. I believe that for a system to last for a long time, it has to be designed around the people who use it! When you begin with how you actually use your home instead of how you've been told you should be using it, you will gain essential insight that will inform your organizational choices.

So often we feel enslaved to the chaos in our homes. Just today I spoke with Sylvia, who has a junk room in her basement and feels trapped inside until she can tackle it. Sylvia shared that when her husband goes out of town, she feels compelled to go down to that room and plug away at the problem. Instead of enjoying her hobbies and friends and family, she is acting as her own jail guard! When her husband comes home from a weekend of fun and relaxation, she emerges from her cell. If you've ever felt you're serving your own mess, now is the time to finally make your home serve you, not the other way around!

By applying the essential discovery process, principles, strategies, and methodologies I've shared with you, you can create a home that suits your lifestyle and serves your needs. Regardless of what season of life you are in, you can set up your home to meet your current demands. Organizing is about making room in your life for what matters to you now—not what used to matter to you, or what might matter to you in the future.

Benefits of Organizing

Reclaim Control

You will gain innumerable benefits from your organizing journey. First, you'll finally begin to reclaim control. You'll begin to experience relief as your household comes under your command and you become an empowered home manager and self-manager. The organizing process strengthens personal boundaries as you become more proactive with your time and less reactive to the circumstances of life. This improved self-management not only feels good, it's a wonderful skill to model and teach your family. An orderly, sane household is a wonderful training ground and gives you and your family a safe home base.

Practice Stewardship

Your organizing process will include pruning back the overage and deadwood in your environment. As you eliminate extraneous belongings and commitments you'll begin to live less wastefully and more mindfully. The founding principle of all my work as a professional organizer is good stewardship. Quite practically, when you are organized, you become a better steward of your environment, belongings, resources, time, and finances. Looking to the needs of others, you can part with your excess and become a blessing at the same time!

Enjoy Freedom

When you no longer feel enslaved to your home, you can begin to shift your inward, survival-mode self-focus to an outward, other-centered focus. Restoring order to your home will allow you to breathe again as you begin to experience freedom from chaos. Peace will begin to descend on your home. When you are living with more order and clarity, you are more prepared to keep your commitments to yourself and to others, thereby fortifying your relationships. You are more able to enjoy the gift of your relationships when you are thinking and living clearly. When your day-to-day living comes into sync with your true values, your lifestyle comes into congruence with your priorities. You and your loved ones will be the beneficiaries of your organizing efforts!

Engaging in an authentic organizing process in your home, then, will actually begin to change *you!* It will set you free from the jail of disorder and release you into freedom.

RESTORING ORDER®
Reclaim Your Life!®

Info@RestoringOrder.com
888.625.5774
www.RestoringOrder.com

To book Vicki Norris, visit:
BookVickiNorris.com

To hire a Restoring Order®
Professional Organizer, visit:
HireRestoringOrder.com

To become a Restoring Order®
Professional Organizer,* visit:
RestoringOrderTraining.com